EXPERT PROFILES

VOLUME 3

Conversations with Influencers & Innovators

EXPERT PROFILES
VOLUME 3
Conversations with Influencers & Innovators

Featuring

Dr. Michael J. Berlin

Nick Jensen

Ryan Comeau, D.C.

David Edwards

Cherie D. Morris

Jennifer M. Segura

Amanda D. Singer

Adrienne Rothstein Grace

Ty Robinson

Expert Profiles Volume 3 – 1st ed.
ISBN: 978-1-946694-14-0

Royalties from the Retail Sales of "Expert Profiles" are
donated to Global Autism Project

AUTISM KNOWS NO BORDERS;
FORTUNATELY NEITHER DO WE.®

Global Autism Project 501(c)3, is a nonprofit organization
which provides training to local individuals in evidence-based
practices for individuals with autism.

Global Autism Project believes that every child has the
ability to learn and their potential should not be limited by
geographical bounds.

The Global Autism Project seeks to eliminate the disparity
in service provision seen around the world by providing high-
quality training to individuals providing services in their local
community. This training is made sustainable through regular
training trips and contiguous remote training.

You can learn more about Global Autism Project by
visiting GlobalAutismProject.org.

Table of Contents

Owner of
The Family Wellness Center,
Chiropractor in Plainview, NY

Dr. Michael J. Berlin is a well-known speaker/educator, has been a wellness coach for thousands of people, and is a fully trained group facilitator. Dr. Berlin practices nutrition, weight loss, stress resolution, and holistic chiropractic in Plainview, NY. Dr. Berlin has dedicated his life to helping people live the Miracle that they are!

Conversation with Dr. Michael J. Berlin

What led you to start The Family Wellness Center?

Dr. Michael J. Berlin: Well, ever since I was little I always marveled at the miracle of life. I just did. I loved nature. I used to sit on the top of trees for hours and sit on ant hills and watch the ants working together. I always marveled at the miracle of life. And so, as I grew I just did things naturally. I ate natural foods. I never took any medicines. And eventually, I knew I wanted to help people. So, as I grew up and I started moving into my career, I brought the two together. And now I'm promoting natural health and the miracle of nature, and life itself, and helping people experience that!

What are you finding in the industry right now with your patients that is a good trend of needs that you're addressing?

Dr. Michael J. Berlin: Well, the most significant need Mike is stress which is the number one killer in our society. According to the Center for Disease Control, they say that 93% of all doctor's visits are stress related. I heard another statistic that said 96%, but we'll go with the lower one.

So, stress is the primary killer, and what we have are two unique protocols that to help people to reverse the effects of stress on their bodies and in their lives. The first one is highly advanced neurological and energy work that clears stress patterns from the spine and nerves; in a way that teaches the body how to eventually do it on its own. And then we have also all natural, holistic nutrition and weight loss that reverses people's weight problems forever!

Basically, what happens is stress comes in three flavors, I say. It comes in physical stresses on the body; which may include jolts, lifting, sitting all day, car accidents, etc. There are chemical stresses such as drugs, pollution, bad food, and medications; anything that's toxic to the body. And of course, there are emotional stresses which we're all familiar with. And all three accumulate over time in the body, particularly in the spine and nervous system. With our methods, we have a way to clear that all out.

And stress and toxins will also lodge in other parts of the body and start to ruin our digestive system and other organs, and we begin to store fat. But we have a way to get that all clean and pristine and get the body back totally; physically, chemically, and emotionally all back to as clear as possible.

Going back to what we started saying, in my perspective nature needs no help; it just needs no interference. We were born healthy and health is our birthright. We're born a miracle. When a baby's born, we say, "Oh, it's a miracle!" Well, we're still that miracle. And so, what happens is that these stresses and toxins interfere with our body function and expression of life. With our expression and *experience* of life. So essentially, what we do with these two extraordinary processes that we do in our office is we clear away and remove all that's interfering with our natural expression of health and life. Then the body miraculously comes back on its own; big time. Because that is the way it is designed.

How do you advise your patients with your techniques and your holistic approach to balance their day-to-day life?

Dr. Michael J. Berlin: That's a great question, Mike. The real truth is that stress is not the problem. It's not stress that causes our body and minds to break down. It is when we cannot adapt to stress correctly, and this causes the body and mind to break down. It's how we adapt to it physically and emotionally. There are lots of examples. If the two of us were in a board meeting and the boss comes in and starts yelling at us because deadlines weren't met, and I get all upset. I'm like, "he shouldn't have talked to us like that. That's not okay. And you know what, he must apologize. I'm not going to be okay with it until he apologizes." I'm creating stress for myself.

Whereas you're sitting next to me, and you're thinking to yourself; "Man, I hope he's okay. I wonder if he's alright. I'm going to go ask him and see if everything's okay with him and what I can do to help." Same situation and two different ways to respond. One causes stress and isolation for me, and the other causes compassion and relationship for you.

How about the people that handle stress differently, potentially even the person that explodes and they get all upset? What are some red flags that someone can notice in their own life that would make them think, "You know, I wonder if Dr. Michael J. Berlin could help with this?"

Dr. Michael J. Berlin: To answer your question accurately… what happens is that stress affects our nervous system, emotional stress. It's how we process it. It's how we perceive, interpret, and respond to stress through our nervous system; including the mind.

The key is to do that authentically because the more authentic we can be in any moment, the more truthful, the more real we can be in any moment, the more we can flow with life. Otherwise, something inside of us goes, "No, this isn't right for me. I'm not handling this right for me. I don't know what to do," and it creates stress.

So, what we do is we help people to become more authentic. We support people's nervous systems physically and emotionally. I know for me if I'm not getting my nervous system cleared on a regular basis and stress is accumulating, for me, the subtle things are that I don't find solutions to problems as quickly. I tend to get irritated a little faster. I can't express myself as much.

But it may not be as subtle. It could be you start getting sick. You have digestive issues, inflammatory bowel disease, spinal problems, back and neck issues, headaches, autoimmune problems. You could have all kinds of stress conditions that you may not even know it's stress.

Essentially, you feel sick and tired, and you're tired of being sick and tired. That would be the epitome of it. And anywhere along the spectrum. So, you're just not functioning at your best. You're not free. You're not happy. You're not powerful. You're not healthy. You're not authentic in your life.

You brought up an interesting point about noticing what stress or your body was doing when you said trouble making decisions. I would suspect that's a perfect correlation to what you just mentioned about the body and keeping your nervous system and your spine as top-notch as possible.

Dr. Michael J. Berlin: That's very accurate. But here's the unfortunate thing. Stress accumulates over our lifetime, from when we were young. It could start from the birthing process. Most people don't know what "clear" feels like. Most people don't even know when they're not clear because we're so stressed, and everybody around us is stressed. We think that's normal. But what happens is when people come in, and they start to clear the interference from their natural expression of life and health, and they go to a whole new level, they say, "Oh my God. I never knew I could be so calm. I never knew I could be so healthy. I didn't know that I could be so expressive and alive."

Now they have a new level of "clear". And so, when that happens, once you know what's right, then you know when you're going off.

That's a great point. You might think, Wow, I had a great day today. Well, compared to what? Well, other days that were bad.

To your point, if stress and this kind of cloudy, cluttered feelings have been building up our entire life, how do we even know what it should feel like because it's been so long, and it's been so gradual?

Dr. Michael J. Berlin: That's right. But what makes our office so unique is that we help people genuinely find and heal the causes of their weight or health problems and reverse them for life. As I said, we have two very powerful processes that heal people, that cleans out the physical, chemical, and emotional stresses that have accumulated over the years. Also, one of my gifts is diagnosis. I see and understand systems very well. It's just something that I do.

I say to people all the time, I coined the phrase, "Stop treating symptoms and start treating *systems*," because we are a bunch of *systems* all within a system that works systematically, and you cannot treat just one part. Everything's connected in our body and in our life, and our body to our life. And so, what makes us unique is that we genuinely find and heal ALL the causes that allow your systems not to function like they're supposed to.

Then, what we do physically, chemically, and emotionally is help the systems reverse all the damage; all the stress and toxicity; clear the interference, and then the body will naturally heal itself. According to research, about 200% better. The body will naturally start healing itself, the body and mind, and become more whole. As I stated, it is designed that way.

More specifically, how we do that is with two processes, one's called Network Spinal Analysis. What that is, is we're trained as chiropractors, but we went back to school, a lot of post-graduate work, to learn a unique form of healing that blends highly advanced neurological and energy work. It's light pressure points. We don't the traditional bone cracking like most chiropractors. It's light pressure points that literally clears out the stress patterns from the spine and nervous system; in a way that also teaches the body how to stay clear on its own.

Then the other system we use is all-natural nutrition and weight loss that reverses the weight problem completely and permanently because there are ten things that need to heal in order to get permanent weight loss. Not just to lose weight, but to permanently remedy the weight problem. If you don't heal all 10, then your weight problem will return; and sometimes with a vengeance. But if you do heal all 10, then you will go back to your natural, healthy weight and stay there. Some of those 10 things are hormones, proper food combining, stress, emotional eating, and toxicity; just to name a few. We offer nutritional programs that completely heal the digestive system and reverses all 10 causes of fat storing. We use only natural food and supplements. We teach people how to shop, cook, and eat; we have life coaching and all-natural spa services that melts fat and naturally contours the body. We guarantee our clients that it will be the last weight loss program that they will ever do!

So, we use those two processes to help people... Like we say, "live the miracle that they are!"

About Dr. Michael J. Berlin

Dr. Michael J. Berlin is trained as a highly skilled and talented healer and communicator. Noted as a gentle, intuitive, and gifted healer, he brings to the community over 25 years of experience working in health care and mind-body healing. Dr. Michael J. Berlin is a well-known speaker/educator, has been a wellness coach for thousands of people, and is a fully trained group facilitator. Dr. Michael J. Berlin practices nutrition, weight loss, stress resolution, and holistic chiropractic in Plainview, NY. Dr. Michael J. Berlin has dedicated his life to helping people live the Miracle that they are!

For a free consultation with Dr. Michael J. Berlin to help you de-stress your body or obtain permanent weight loss, please go to: www.NetworkWellnessCenter.com or call 516-822-8499

The Financial Cowboy

Nick Jensen, the Financial Cowboy, is no stranger to hard work, rough play, and working with folks to create wealth and hold on to it. He's a former bull rider turned business and financial professional, who helps people create strategies that allow them to eliminate debt, build wealth outside of Wall Street, prepare for a tax-advantaged retirement, and leave a family legacy. His mission and purpose are to empower those who want to change their financial future and change their family's legacy for the better, with the knowledge and strategies they need to do so.

Nick's earliest memories are growing up on his grandfather's farm he homesteaded in Idaho. This is where he learned to work and to play, it's where he learned to raise springer heifers and where he dreamed of becoming a World Champion Bull Rider someday. After many years of chasing rodeos through high school, college and eventually the PRCA, Nick's life took an academic turn.

The pain of not rodeoing anymore caused Nick to bury himself in school, obtaining a Bachelor of Science degree and Master of Business Administration. Since 2004, Nick has spent much of his career in the finance world unraveling Wall Street's deceptions.

As a financial expert and podcaster, Nick now works to help hard-working families achieve the financial freedom they want and deserve, worry free.

Conversation with Nick Jensen

Nick, you talk about real wealth-building strategies that really work for real people, can you tell me about the Financial Cowboy and how you are helping your clients?

Nick Jensen: As you know, I am a former professional bull rider, that was several years ago, back in the day. And after that career, I went to school and got into the finance world, so I've been kind of through the gamut of everything that Wall Street has to offer. I started some businesses, made a bunch of money, lost a bunch of money, and through all that process have gained some valuable knowledge to help individuals really learn how to build wealth.

The kind of wealth that the richest and wealthiest families in America build, not the kind of wealth that Wall Street wants to think you can have by investing in the products that you see on the media and touted by financial entertainers, if you will. Solid-based strategies that are long-term and really allow individuals to implement them step by step without taking tons of risk.

Many people have problems with money from the get-go. What is one problem that you specialize in solving that almost everyone is going to have?

Nick Jensen: I think the education that we receive oftentimes around finances comes from the media and the things that the media touts are what they're getting paid to tout. It's marketing budgets, it's who's paying us dollars for us to get the revenue that we need to have our shows on the TV, right?

When you think of the media and you think of the things that we're learning or where we're learning those things, and it's not just TV, it's radio, it's the magazines and things of that nature. All those dollars, if you really chased those back, those are going back to Wall Street or they're coming from Wall Street. What everybody faces, is where do I put my dollar? When I earn a dollar, where do I put that dollar to accumulate more dollars?

Well, Wall Street wants you to put it with them, whether that's through a brokerage account or through a government-funded or government-sponsored 401K or 403B, which has its issues and problems, but that's probably a story for another day.

Those are the choices you have. Where do I put this dollar? And so, the thing that everybody faces is, without understanding real true financial principles and how to really build wealth, they go straight to Wall Street and they go to either a mutual fund or an exchange-traded fund or buying stocks or bonds or something of that nature, but that all goes back to Wall Street.

How does that benefit everybody? Or how does that benefit the investor? You've got the potential to make money if you know exactly when to buy and when to sell and don't get wrapped up in all the emotions - which studies have been done, that's nearly impossible to do.

Wall Street is going to collect fees from you whether you're making money or not, and that's how Wall Street exists. And when I say Wall Street, I'm talking about money managers, I'm talking about mutual funds, I'm talking about financial advisors like myself. I'm talking about big brokerage firms. The way they make money is by charging you fees, whether you make money or not.

That's the problem that everybody's facing is, how do I get my capital to grow without it being chewed up in fees and not taking on too much risk? It's kind of this risk and control thing, right? You want to take on the least amount of risk as possible and have the ultimate amount of control as possible, and what everybody faces or the challenge that everybody faces when they go to Wall Street, that's completely opposite. They take on the ultimate amount of risk and have the least amount of control. The idea is how do you get around that? How do you solve that?

Maybe people don't know what to do with their money, but then are they afraid they can't be sure their advisor is doing the right thing?

Nick Jensen: The problem is you don't know if they're doing the right thing. Think about it this way. A popular company right now is Apple, right? If you say Apple, everybody knows what that is. The iPads, the iPhones and things like that.

Think about this, if you've got $10,000, or $100,000, or $1,000,000, it doesn't matter...the dollar amount doesn't matter. But let's say that you go to your local brokerage firm and you hand them a check for, let's just call it $100,000 and you say, "I want to invest this in Apple" okay?

When you look at the risk and control spectrum, you hand your brokerage firm that check to invest in Apple. You have zero control over the outcome of that investment. You're beholding to the board of directors at Apple making good decisions, you're beholding to Tim Cook not doing something stupid or scandalous, and Apple itself continuing to add value to the marketplace in which people want to continue to buy their products and therefore increase the value of the company.

You have zero control over what happens there and because you have no control, you're at the ultimate height of risk, if you will. Because let's say that Tim Cook does something stupid or let's say that Apple is no longer able to add value to the marketplace and the stock plummets. You've got the ultimate amount of risk. There is nothing that you can do as an investor to affect the outcome of that investment. Zero! There's nothing you can do. You could sell, right? You could sell your investment for a loss if you want, or you could hold on to it and hope that it comes back, but there's nothing that you can do to affect the outcome of the way that Apple performs.

What are the advantages of staying away from Wall Street, and what are the strategies you like to talk about? How do we get started doing that?

Nick Jensen: Here are the advantages of staying away from Wall Street. It goes back to risk and control. By staying away from Wall Street...and Wall Street has its place, as long as it's in the proper context and invested in at the appropriate time, it has its place. What I'm against, is that's the first place that everybody goes and that's really the last place everybody should go. Okay?

The advantages of staying away from Wall Street are this: if you do it properly...the way that I build out strategies for clients, is I follow this framework that I call the Wealth Haystack.

Think of it as a layered approach. The first thing you do is you invest in the bottom layer. The bottom layer you're going to have the very least amount of risk that you can have with your money and you're going to have the ultimate amount of control over your money. Once you build that layer out and that layer is solid, only then do you go to the next layer. And the next layer above that you're going to allocate a smaller portion of your portfolio to that layer.

Because what you don't want to have happen is, if something happens in the above layer, let's just say the above layer collapses, you don't want it to affect the layer below. You always want to have the solid foundation, the solid base. So, layer number two or the second layer is hard assets. Things you can touch, things you can feel, things you have control over.

When you go to that second layer, you're going to be taking on a little bit more risk. There is no doubt. You're also going to be giving up just a little bit of control. That's inevitable, but you're doing it at the appropriate time.

The next layer is hard assets and hard assets...there's mainly two that I tell people to invest in. One is real estate because we know when we look at wealth and the way that wealth has been built and wealthy families and generational wealth, real estate is a huge component of that process. So, one of the hard assets is real estate, and cash flowing real estate, meaning that it's creating revenue for you. It's not necessarily investing in real estate to just hold capital, you know, as an inflation hedge, but actually investing in real estate that kicks off a cash flow to you. So that's number one.

Rental properties, storage units, apartment buildings, farmland if you know how to create cash flow from farmland, ranches, things of that nature, things that you can touch and feel. If the economy completely collapses, you have a hard asset that is worth something, right?

That's number one. The second thing is business and not just any business, but your business. So, it's one of those situations where it's a business/invest in yourself scenario - meaning that if you start a business, you have a lot of control over the outcome of that business. Yes, there's going to be some factors out of your control, but you have a lot of control as to how that business is going to perform.

If it's not performing well, there's things that you can personally do to try to help that business perform better. Right? You are taking on a little bit more risk, but here again, you have a lot of control over what happens there. So, that's mainly the other second component in the hard asset pieces.

You've got cash flowing real estate and you've got businesses. Those are the next two things that you would invest in.

If someone is investing in their own business, it doesn't have to be a large business, right? Could this be a home-based small business that's going to have tax advantages, much like real estate does?

Nick Jensen: Yes. There's tax advantages to real estate and there's tax advantages to having your own business. There are going to be different tax advantages, but yes, there are tax advantages to both. And you're correct. When you think about your own business, it doesn't have to be this big elaborate five hundred employee company.

It could be a side hustle. It could be a home-based business. It could be a network marketing business if you want. I'm not a huge fan of that industry, but it can be anything like that, that would allow you to generate more revenue and give you some tax advantages but also allowing you to have control over what's happening versus not taking on too much risk.

And you never know what's going to happen with your job or with your health or something, because that is out of your control. But if you had that side hustle or a small business you could grow quickly if you had to, if it was a proven business model that was working, you'd be in a much better position, correct?

Nick Jensen: You're 100% correct. And that's one of the misconceptions or one of the fallacies that we live with today, "Oh, I've got a good job, I'm secure." No, you're not. Go ask your neighbor who's been laid off before. One day they think they're secure and everything's going well. The next day they find out that the job that they've just spent ten years at, laid them off and now they've got to kind of reinvent themselves or regroup. So yes, you're 100% right. You never know what's going to happen. Having your own type of business, whether it's a side hustle or a part-time business, is definitely advantageous. And I would encourage everybody, regardless of their situation, I would encourage everybody to have something in their hip pocket that allows them to generate extra revenue.

Look in the marketplace and say, "Okay, what are my particular skills? Where can I add value in the marketplace?" and then start a business around that. I've got a good friend of mine, he loves mowing lawns, it's kind of his solace. It's what he likes to do. Two or three years ago, he started a lawn mowing business in which he just put out some flyers, that he's got this business out there and if they're interested, give him a call. Well, the first year he got somewhat busy. The second year he got really busy and then he added aerating and then the third year, all of a sudden, he's pulling around this trailer with his logo on it and he's got these big riding lawn mowers.

Yes, he's still got a full-time job, but he started this side hustle that if he's not careful, he's going to have to make a choice. Do I stay with my full-time job or do I just grow my own business? Simply because he liked to mow lawns.

I know someone who started a cleaning business. And she got so busy with referrals she didn't do any advertising or promotion. She didn't want employees, she didn't want a big business, she just wanted to keep that little side hustle gig and keep her good clients. Could it grow into a real business if she lost her regular job and that's what she needed to do?

Nick Jensen: Sure, absolutely, and here's a little tidbit. If you want to grow your business and you want to grow the economic value of your business, when you get to the point where you must expand, just raise your prices.

Because as you raise your prices, all of a sudden, your value goes up and you're going to be able to make more money doing the same amount of work, or you're going to get busier because now all of a sudden, you're more expensive so people feel like you're more valuable and your client base increases.

Do you see some of the most common fears that people face by keeping their money out of Wall Street, so to speak, like keeping it in a more controllable fashion - real estate, is it overwhelming for them?

Nick Jensen: It depends on the individual. It can seem overwhelming, but it's like anything else. If you haven't been there before, it's scary, right? Our mental capacity, our minds, where do we always revert to? We always revert to what's comfortable, what's familiar. Well, in our minds, from an investing standpoint, what is comfortable? What is familiar? Well, investing in 401K is comfortable. My HR departments talked about it, everybody else does it. The stock market, that's familiar. I understand - I buy a stock and I sell a stock. If the market goes up, I make money. If the market goes down, I lose money. That's comfortable, that's familiar.

Do people have some apprehension about maybe investing in hard assets? Yeah, a little bit because unless their family has done it, or they know somebody else has done it, there are some things you're going to have to learn. And when you look at real estate, there's so many different aspects that you can invest in, right? You can focus on turnkey properties, you can find a provider out there and there's a ton of them that offer great value, that allow you to buy a piece of property and then they'll manage that property for you.

You basically are buying the property, they're putting tenants in, they're sending you rent checks every month and you're paying them a fee to do so, right? You can go from there to all the way up to a pooled type investment, to where you've got four or five or fifty or a hundred investors taking down a large project.

There's so many ways that you can invest in real estate. But yes, some people have mental blocks on what that looks like and maybe they don't want to deal with it, but there's ways around all those scenarios, depending on how dirty you want to get your hands, right? If you want to get your hands dirty, then you flip houses, right?

Like you go buy the biggest piece of junk house in an okay neighborhood and you start swinging a hammer. And then that's a way that you can make money.

Getting back to the Haystack, layer number two is hard assets, right? So, real estate and your own business. The next layer is alternative investments. So, these are investments that you're going to lose some control, meaning you're not going to have any control over the outcome of that investment, but they're not tied to Wall Street. So, let me give you a couple examples.

Maybe it's an oil and gas lease type venture, so it's a land lease on oil and gas in which you've invested in this oil and gas scenario, which has tax advantages, by the way, just being invested in oil and gas, there's some certain tax advantages to that, and then you're collecting a check.

Depending on the type of investment, if it's a land lease, you're going to basically collect a check because they're renting the land from you to drill for oil and gas, or if you invest in actual oil and gas production, that's a different type of investment. But it's not tied to Wall Street, right? It's an investment outside of Wall Street.

So that's one example. Another example, this is interesting, and you can get creative in the alternative assets space. I know a guy who was lending money on semi-trucks. He did it one time for a friend and then word got around, so it just kind of grew and perpetuated. And I don't understand the semi-truck business 100%, but I'll give you what I know. My understanding is, to buy a semi-truck, you can either go to the bank and get a loan, or Peterbilt or Kenworth will finance the truck for you, right?

It's probably like auto financing at the dealership. It's going to be a little bit higher or you're going to pay a premium for that financing, right? What this guy did, is he filled the gap for people that couldn't get a loan at the bank but really couldn't buy their own truck by paying twelve, fifteen, 20% in order to buy that vehicle, right?

What he would do, is he would require a down payment, I can't remember how much it was. He would be the first lien holder on the truck. He would get the insurance on the vehicle and he would require a truck payment and insurance payment every month from the new owner. Right? And if a payment didn't show up, he would go and repossess the truck. He said he'd never had to go repossess a truck, but he ensured that one - the title was in his name or in his business's name; two - there was insurance on the vehicle because he got the insurance, or made sure the insurance was current.

And three, they were paying him at a fair interest rate. So, they were paying more than they would have to pay at the bank, but not as much as they would have to pay, assuming they did it at through the finance company. So, that's alternative assets, that's another...

Okay, I've got a quick question then. That made me think of something - micro-lending, does that fall under the alternative assets?

Nick Jensen: Yes, like Lending Club is kind of popular right now. You can invest a thousand bucks, $5,000, whatever you want to do, and then you can say what type of investments you want to be in. That would be a type of alternative asset, right? You're losing control over what's going to happen and you're taking on a little bit more risk, but it's not tied to Wall Street.

But here again, every layer you move up, a smaller portion of your portfolio is being allocated to that layer. Let's say that in the alternative asset piece, all of your money was in micro-lending or Lending Club, or whatever the case may be and that completely went away for some reason. Every investment you'd invested in went away, well, you still have your hard assets underneath that and you still have your base layer underneath that.

So, your base layer is cash, cash equivalent type savings accounts, right? And then the last piece would be market-based investment or venture capital type stuff. Like you don't have any control over what happens and you're taking on the ultimate amount of risk. It's one of those situations where you just must know, any money you put in there, - yeah, you've got potential to make money, but you also have the potential of everything to completely go away.

It's "mad money." Is it like when you go to Vegas? Where you're willing to risk losing some money and it won't bother you?

Nick Jensen: Yes. And I'll be the first to admit, the stock market is attractive. It's appealing. One of the things that I love to do is trade futures. I don't do it anymore, just because I'm busy doing other things, but it's an attractive thing to do. I enjoy doing it because of kind of this rush. You make a lot of money fast and then you can lose a lot of money fast and being able to try to time the markets and things like that. That's exciting.

The problem is, is when you look at that long-term, from just a regular investor standpoint, the number of people that get ahead is slim, none and zero.

Right, and is this usually beyond your average family guy with three kids and a job and a side hustle? I mean, he's busy.

Nick Jensen: Yes, and here again you're 100% right. I would never tell any of my clients, "Hey, you should start day trading futures," or "Hey, you should start putting money in this computer-based trading." If they're at the point where they're like, "Hey, I've just got so much money, I don't know what to do with it, I think I want to go to the stock market," then it's going to be more of a, "Okay, let's look at some legacy type stocks," and when I say legacy type stock, look at it like a value type investment.

When the market crashes, when there's blood in the street, let's look at some companies that have historically paid decent dividends. Let's buy those companies up and then it doesn't matter if the stock goes up, down or sideways, hopefully we're going to get a dividend off of that, but it's not a situation in which we're buying, hoping or praying that the market goes up, because if it doesn't go well, if we're going to lose all of our money, we're just not doing that, right?

It's just a matter of, okay, where's some value out there that pays some dividends that we can hold some cash, knowing that the tax advantages of doing stuff like that are not very good? And when you kind of think about this hierarchical structure, I know multiple millionaires that go to the second layer - real estate and their own business, and that's as far as they go. They don't invest in anything else but those two things, and they make gobs and gobs and gobs of money.

It's all about acquiring as many assets as possible because when you start to look at this from a generational standpoint, it's this idea between the finite game and the infinite game, right?

Simon Sinek did a TED Talk back in 2015 on game theory and he talked about this finite game versus this infinite game. I think oftentimes we look at investing as a finite game, meaning defined players, defined rules, I've got to win. Whereas an infinite game is unknown players, unknown rules and I got to stay in the game and staying in the game is, I got to acquire enough wealth, not just for me to retire, but to set my kids up and then hopefully to teach them that they can use that wealth to create more wealth and set my grandkids up, and so on and so forth, than this wealth just perpetuates down the ages and you know, four or five generations down the road, all of a sudden your last name is synonymous with the Rockefellers.

I was just thinking about how different people might just stick with a couple different layers within the haystack, but it's situational dependent on when someone is going to move past that first layer up to the next layer, right?

Nick Jensen: That's a great point and that's exactly what I do. When I bring on a new client, it's all about sitting down figuring out, "Okay, what are you currently doing? What are your biggest pain points and what levers can we pull to help you be more efficient?" And so that all boils down to, okay, looking at the base layer, where are we at? What do we need to add to that base layer to move to the next layer? By knowing what that is, then we can determine when to move to the next layer.

And this is all about building wealth, right? Because the idea is once you build the wealth out, when you hit retirement, you've got to then reverse that and start to take an income from that wealth. It's a strategy of building it all out. Then when you hit retirement, taking the cash flow from it, and then the third piece is when you die, because unfortunately we're all going to die at some point, how do I efficiently pass that on to the next generation?

It's all about how you do it, timing of when to do it, being able to strategize on what that looks like and making the current dollars that we have become the most efficient.

Now it's never too late to start your haystack, right? If someone's thinking, "Man, I'm just too old. What do I do now? I don't have time."... What's the easiest way to get started?

Nick Jensen: I think the easiest way is you must take action, right? You must do something. It goes back to the old analogy: when was the best time to plant a tree? Well, twenty years ago. Okay, well when's the second-best time? Today! It doesn't matter if you're twenty years old or seventy years old, you've got to do something, and everybody in between is going to be at a different stage in life and therefore their strategy is probably going to look a little bit differently. The strategy for a sixty-five-year-old with no assets versus the strategy for a sixty-five-year-old with a ton of assets is two different strategies.

If you're in a position where you're like, "You know what? I know I need help, but I don't want to do it on my own, but I need some guidance." That's when you reach out to somebody that you can trust, that you feel like is going to give you good financial advice and understand.

There's already this stigma that you feel like you walk into a financial adviser's office and it's like a used car lot, right? "Don't let him out the door!" type scenario and that's not the environment you want to be in.

There's tons of free education out there that you can go to. You can go to thefinancialcowboy.com, I've got some blog posts. If you want to know more about the wealth haystack, you can go to the financialcowboy.com/haystack. You can download the PDF on the wealth haystack, that'll give you a structure you can start to follow.

And if you want specific help for your specific situation, go to the website and feel free to schedule a free consultation with me. I'll be honest with you during that consultation. If I can help you, I'll tell you what that looks like. If I can't help you, I'll probably either tell you I can't help you or I'll refer you somebody that I think can, but at the end of the day you've got to decide, do you want to tackle this on your own or do you want some professional advice to help you tackle it?

About Nick Jensen

Nick Jensen, The Financial Cowboy, is a financial services expert who helps people build wealth that lasts for generations.

He's seen poor financial strategies eventually force the sale of his grandpa's farm, he's seen Wall Street take the life savings of hard working people leaving families desolate and a rising generation not knowing how to create generational wealth through practical planning. If you're a farmer, rancher, professional cowboy, business owner or simply a hard-working American wanting to grow and keep your wealth outside of the confines of Wall Street and the Government, Nick believes he has some insight and experiences that can help make an incredible impact in your family's legacy.

When he's not working, Nick spends most of his free time with his wife and kids. Although their childhood is different than his, he wants them to look back on his family's legacy as a great experience.

WEBSITE
www.TheFinancialCowboy.com

EMAIL
nick@thefinancialcowboy.com

LOCATION
132 Pierpont Ave
Salt Lake City, Utah 84103

FACEBOOK
@thefinancialcowboy

TWITTER
@financecowboy

PHONE
801-262-5030

How Kinetisense is Revolutionizing the Rehabilitation and Movement Therapies Industries

Dr. Ryan Comeau is CEO and co-founder of Kinetisense. Dr. Comeau is considered a world leader and pioneer in the field of human 3D motion capture. Dr. Comeau is an innovator, best-selling author, and advocate for the implementation of objectivity and patient engagement in the health sciences. Dr. Comeau is an international speaker and shares his vision for how technology will forever change rehabilitation, movement therapies, and the healthcare system in general.

The developer of motion analysis software for life science industries. This patented product allows for accurate, efficient and objective range of motion and movement analysis of patients. Kinetisense practitioners can acquire accurate movement data by means of infrared camera technology without the use of wearable sensors.

Kinetisense has revolutionized the way that rehab practitioners and fitness trainers acquire and assess human bio- mechanical data. Kinetisense has combined award-winning practitioners and a Microsoft MVP development team to produce a patented motion-capture assessment tool.

Conversation with Ryan Comeau, D.C.

Can you tell us about Kinetisense and how it helps people move better?

Ryan Comeau: Absolutely. Kinetisense is a 3D motion capture system that uses a single front-facing camera and is objective, portable, efficient, and allows for the acquisition of movement data of the patient, the client. The system allows for the accurate assessment of human biomechanics, which allows for physiotherapists, chiropractors, trainers, coaches, and researchers to objectively analyze and correct movement patterns.

Kinetisense has developed a technology that is used in functional movement assessment, sports performance, from professional athletes all the way down to amateur in grade school. Practitioners are also using it to assess the risk of a fall in the geriatric population. Properly assessing this risk enables practitioners to apply the appropriate protection mechanisms or rehabilitation to prevent the fall. Corporate wellness, research, and education also use Kinetisense.

Kinetisense has created a multi-based or module-based platform comprised of Kinetisense movement assessment modules; and, we've also brought in third-party developed modules, such as Kinetisport, the application of 3D motion capture for analyzing sports-specific movements.

Ryan, to help people visualize what Kinetisense is like, and how a patient might experience it in a practitioner's office, could you describe that process and how Kinetisense works?

Ryan Comeau: Kinetisense uses a single front-facing camera. It started off with the Microsoft Xbox camera, which many people understand because it is the technology used in the gaming world. Until now, a lot of practitioners and trainers would have to eyeball their assessments or use these archaic plastic tools.

Instead of those old tools, the patient now stands in front of the 3D motion-sensing camera and Kinetisense has created a software system that will pick up the joints of the body immediately. The patient or the client will see themselves on a screen in real time with all the joints marked, lit up, and the respective range of motion of those joints as they go through the prescribed exercises.

We also represent motion in three planes. It's almost like having a practitioner standing in front of you, standing beside you, and hovering over top of you all at once. You can see how without technology such as this, without being able to engage the patient, the client, with the visuals, it's very hard to get objective data. We're very limited as practitioners, as trainers. Not having objective data affects the overall quality of care.

Why are chiropractors, physical therapists, performance coaches, and trainers, and even technologists, so interested in being involved with Kinetisense?

Ryan Comeau: It comes down to the problem that we're trying to solve. There's a major gap that exists between what we see at the clinical grade human motion capture systems; systems such as the VICON system and comparing that to the tools and technologies that the practitioners and the movement specialists have in their clinics or their gyms.

Systems like the VICON, which is an eight-camera system mounted to the ceiling, where you have the patient or the client wearing a suit with the markers, these systems are great for research. We see these in university biomechanical labs, but they have an enormous cost. Some of these biomechanical labs can cost upwards to three, four million dollars. The space requirement is tremendous, and considerable calibration time required.

Kinetisense is an affordable and portable system that analyzes joint angles and joint planes in real time without having any of the calibrations, and with a system that's incredibly affordable. The practitioners can afford this. The trainers can afford this in the gyms. Even the patient can afford to have a system in their own home.

Practitioners and movement specialists no longer must rely on eyeballing their assessments or using assessment tools that have been proven to lack inter-examiner reliability and overall accuracy. It's quite crazy the *gold standards* that we have for analyzing a joint range of motion, the goniometer and inclinometers, were developed and invented in the late 1800s, and we are still using them. There's a massive gap that exists, and we're trying to close that gap quickly with technology such as Kinetisense.

How does Kinetisense bridge that gap?

Ryan Comeau: Kinetisense bridges the gap by producing or creating a technology that can give us the level of accuracy of systems like the VICON; and be able to have the reproducibility with every assessment. We provide standardization to the assessment so that every time one or multiple practitioners analyze a patient or client, it's the same joint, it's reproducible, and the data is valid.

The great thing is, is until now, the technology to acquire 3D motion was not available to most practitioners. We had to rely on expensive, huge, cumbersome systems that did not work and were not feasible for the clinic setting, or for the training setting. We had to use outdated plastic handheld tools instead. However, most practitioners don't even use those tools. They eyeball an assessment which is incredibly subjective.

Because of the technology that Kinetisense uses was available to the masses, it's affordable. These 3D cameras cost anywhere between $150 to $300. They're incredibly affordable. Then, with the Kinetisense system, we're able to allow the trainers, the practitioners to have a biomechanics lab, so to speak, in their clinic, or in their training facility. That's how we're bridging the gap. We're allowing this high-quality research grade type of instrument to be used by all.

What are some of the misconceptions people may have about using technology in their practice to help them measure and monitor movement?

Ryan Comeau: When we're talking about healthcare practitioners, we're talking about gold standards. Gold standards also apply to the fitness world as well. We get stuck in certain paradigms. We get stuck in using certain tools certain ways. That becomes of our day-to-day clinical or training process. That's the main reason that some may decide not to buy this technology is that they're not willing to move into this new paradigm change.

These practitioners and trainers have been doing assessment a certain way for a certain number of years and are not willing to introduce a novel way of assessment. We find that adding technology scares practitioners because believe there will be a large learning curve, which is, with Kinetisense, not the case.

We are finding that the paradigm of objectivity is starting to take hold. It is taking hold in the health sciences as well as in rehab fitness. Soon, it will be required to have this level of biomechanical data, such as what we present with Kinetisense. We see demand from insurance companies and other groups that require this type of information.

Kinetisense has been designed to be an affordable solution so that it is accessible to all movement specialists; so that it comes down to a change of paradigm and to change the way that we do things.

To illustrate your point, could you share a case study or an example of how Kinetisense helped a practitioner in his or her practice to more effectively run their business, as well as help their patients and clients?

Ryan Comeau: One of the cases that come to mind immediately is with the functional movement assessment. Functional movement screens are the ability to analyze or screen someone's movement by taking them through a series of different movements in different planes and being able to quantify what their dysfunctions are, or what joints, or which planes are not moving properly, and how that pertains to their sports.

These functional movement screens are becoming very popular, but up until now, they were done visually. It's very,

very subjective. The other thing, too, is time. Functional movement screens can take 25 to 30 minutes to do properly.

There has been a shift that has occurred in the rehab and fitness arena where we're starting to try to find the dysfunctions of movement before they create an injury. We want to look at how this affects performance as well.

We had a football team for movement assessments. We have a module in our system called KAMS, the Kinetisense Advanced Movement Screen. In this three-minute functional movement screen, we capture data on all the player's joints. The system will take the player through these different movements, and then score them, and then give information on where the discrepancies in movement are.

We took the whole football team through the process, using a three-minute assessment for each player. It was amazing some of the issues that we would find with the hip, the shoulder. How some of these old injuries that these players had had were still representing themselves in how they move. Even though they weren't in pain anymore, or didn't have any discomfort, or perceived discomfort, or anything like that from their old injuries, it was still affecting their overall performance. They had found ways in their body to compensate. These compensation strategies become locked; they become part of the whole matrix of how the person moves. It affected performance and increasing their risk for future injury.

We saw these trends. Now we're starting to see these data trends in different sports and in the different injuries that we see.

One of the cool cases was one of the football players on the team we assessed who had sustained a concussion. Luckily, we also had done a baseline assessment of his balance. We were able to know what his normal balance numbers were versus just visually looking at his balance.

When he had a concussion, we were then able to reassess and compare to what his baseline numbers were. We were able to go through the process of managing his concussion and getting him safely back on the field once he was back to his baseline numbers.

My point with these examples is the versatility. We provide the versatility of being able to not only analyze and treat patients that are in pain but prevent issues as well. Imagine how our professions would change when we start to treat people before they get pain. We start to fix their underlying movement dysfunctions before it causes an injury. That's what this technology is all about, and that's how we're going to change the paradigm now with sciences.

Are you moving from a reactive illness-based healthcare system to a proactive one where you're able to identify and correct issues or put prescriptive mechanisms in place to prevent injuries from happening in the future?

Ryan Comeau: Exactly. You hit the nail on the head. That's why we believe this technology, or this type of technology will not only change paradigms in chiropractic physiotherapy, fitness training, but we think that this is going to have a huge impact on the healthcare system in general. We are talking about a problem that has become an epidemic of chronic diseases. These diseases are a *movement epidemic* because it is a lifestyle and lack of movement that causes most of the disease that we see that are killing us. We're just not moving anymore, and we're not moving well. We're not moving properly.

This epidemic even reaches into our children. Imagine having a system like this in the gym class, where kids can learn how to move. They have the visual feedback in real time. They can learn how to move better, and they become confident in their movement. That then leads them into loving sports, loving movement, because they have that confidence and it affects them later in life, and hopefully helps to reduce some of these horrible diseases that we're seeing. The prescription is simple. It's called movement.

We can help anyone who wants to improve their movement. Whether it's performance-based and you are a professional athlete. Maybe you are an amateur athlete that wants the edge or wants to stay away from injuries. Perhaps you are someone who's had an injury that needs to rehab it properly, or you are just getting a perspective of how to move and learning to move better. That's what this technology is all about.

What led you to develop Kinetisense?

Ryan Comeau: It's like any invention that we see. Inventors, we'll think up ideas, or inventions will come to fruition obviously to try to fill a gap that exists. Luckily enough, my journey with sports and learning about rehab, I was exposed to this gap that exists with the functional assessment.

To make a long story short, during my undergraduate time, I was lucky enough and honored enough to be able to work in a biomechanics lab. We're talking about these VICON lab systems which were about a three-million-dollar lab and camera system. We were doing incredible research on movement disorders there. Research on things like Parkinson's, and other different issues that people have, and the data was outstanding. Then, that sparked my interest in getting into rehab medicine.

Then, when I was going to chiropractic school, and learning about the different assessment tools that physiotherapists and chiropractors use, I was just absolutely blown away to see that the tools that were employed now were these handheld tools that had been around for hundreds of years.

I stood there in class, and I thought, "This can't be right! Using outdated tools has a huge effect on the practitioner if they want to be objective. How does this affect the patient and their process for going through rehabilitation? How does this affect our healthcare system in general? A healthcare system that's now going broke?" We have no compass. It was my opinion that we had no objective, reliable and standardized method of assessing and monitoring a patient's progress through rehabilitation. The lack of objectivity, accuracy, and standardization was a massive problem.

That's when we started to investigate different ways that we could try to get a high level of biomechanical data but get it to the masses. We knew at that time that the new Xbox camera was coming out. It was a system used for gaming. We were able to apply proprietary algorithms and different coding to accurately assess the joints *without the use of wearables*. Our goal was to provide this technology at an affordable price so that we could have the chiropractors, the physiotherapists, the medical doctors, the researcher, the fitness trainer all able to have a system; and now we're talking about multi-disciplinary health care.

Where instead of them all assessing differently with different tools and using different methods, they're now using a standardized assessment. You can imagine how this now forever changes how we do healthcare, and deliver better outcomes, better patient satisfaction; because we analyze the patient in a standardized way. The healthcare community, the team that he or she has, can share data through the cloud, through HIPAA compliant cloud, obviously, with the sign-off of the patient. Being able to share this information, being able to have a gauge, being able to have a compass, to move, being able to intervene when intervention is required. That's what Kinetisense is all about. That's what our ultimate goal is, and that's the gap that we're trying to fill.

What's the most important question a practitioner or a business owner should ask themselves if they're considering incorporating Kinetisense into their practice?

Ryan Comeau: The main question about incorporating Kinetisense, is to ask, "How is this going to give me the edge?" That *really* is the main question. Consider how it will make you stand out. Is this going to differentiate me, my clinic, from the other clinics that are around me? Am I providing a higher level of care to my patients? Also, am I now able to transform my clinic from a different paradigm. Moving from one that is looking just at rehabilitation of injuries and pain to now one of prevention?

I would argue that a technology such as Kinetisense revolutionizes the clinic, changes the clinic, changes the way that the patient, the practitioner looks at movement. It changes the way that the patient is engaged in their rehab. The beautiful thing about this technology is it is so easy to use.

We've designed it to be so easy to use that everyone in the office can use it from the practitioner to the front desk staff, so efficiency is always there. It even improves efficiency, because it helps to write out many chart notes for the practitioner, or the trainer. You don't even have to go through having to write everything out. It's automatic. It creates reports automatically. Kinetisense is about differentiating. It's about being very good at what we do. Sometimes technology like this could take us to the next level.

If people wanted to learn more about Kinetisense and learn more about you, where should they go?

Ryan Comeau: The best place to learn more about Kinetisense is to go to our website www.Kinetisense.com. We also have a Facebook page, a Kinetisense Facebook page where we share a considerable amount of information, research, and user profiles. We demonstrate different ways of using Kinetisense. Checking us online through our website, or through Facebook is the best way. Our contact information is on there if anyone wants to contact us and have a discussion, to talk, learn more. We are always willing to answer questions and share information.

About Ryan Comeau, D.C.

Dr. Ryan Comeau is a board-certified Chiropractor as well as an acupuncture provider that has an interest in movement rehabilitation and sports performance. Dr. Comeau graduated with honors and distinction from Southern California University of Health Sciences and has acquired new techniques and certifications including acupuncture, Graston, Active Release, and SFMA (selective functional movement analysis) provider.

Prior to his chiropractic education, Dr. Comeau was awarded a Division 1 NCAA hockey scholarship at University of Alaska Fairbanks and finished his Bachelor of Science degree in biological sciences (psychology minor) at the University of Alberta.

Dr. Comeau is CEO and Co-founder of Kinetisense, a 3D motion capture technology that is using used by a variety of practitioners in the field of Parkinson research, Geriatric risk of fall, concussion management, and sports performance. Kinetisense has its international headquarters in Medicine Hat, Alberta.

WEBSITE
www.Kinetisense.com

EMAIL
info@kinetisense.com

LOCATION
133 Markwick Drive SE
Medicine Hat, Alberta, T1A7V9

FACEBOOK
Facebook.com/kinetisense

TWITTER
@kinetisense

INSTAGRAM
@kinetisense

Wealth Advisor
President of Heron Wealth

David Edwards is president and founder of Heron Wealth, which provides financial planning, investment advice, and estate planning services to individuals and families across the United States and in Europe.

David and his experienced wealth advisor team guide their clients to the options that matter most to them and their families. David counsels them on saving for major purchases such as a house, budgeting for your children's education or planning for retirement. In managing his client's investment accounts, David balances investment risk with long-term returns and tax-efficiency.

Founded by President David Edwards in 1996, Heron Wealth currently manages $375 million in client assets. Heron Wealth is a New York City-based, independent wealth advisory firm that provides financial planning, investment advice, and estate planning services to families living in the United States, Europe, and Latin America.

Briefly describe the kinds of people who you serve, and the various types of situations they find themselves in when they reach out to you for your help.

David Edwards: Certainly. We specialize in executive families. That is a typically a two-person household, husband, and wife, or perhaps the same-sex family, a couple of kids going to college. They want that dream retirement. They want that second home. They're somewhat worried about their aging parents. They have literally 10,000 choices. It's our job to guide them to the 10 choices that matter to them most and help them pick the best three.

Okay, Dave, now that we have an idea of who you help, it goes without saying that anything you share with us today is not legal advice, legal assistance, therapeutic assistance, or any other kind of advice. It's purely for the purposes of disseminating information. Could expand on that in your own words, so everybody's clear of what we're doing today?

David Edwards: Sure. I am giving general advice about financial planning, investment advice, and estate planning. Of course, you should always consult with an appropriately credentialed advisor on any of those topics before you make your own decisions.

When you think about the executive families you help, what's their most common misconception about the glide path to retirement?

David Edwards: The most common misconception is that you can postpone dealing with your retirement until the day that you retire. In our mind, that's like a pilot flying into

Kennedy, but instead of making a decision 30 minutes out to reduce the airspeed, and light up the runway, and start gently gliding down to the airport, and lowering and locking the landing gear, it's almost like they ride at 35,000, and then just drop down to the runway from directly above.

There are both financial issues to be addressed in retirement, and also emotional issues to be addressed in retirement, such as are we going to stay in this home? Are we going to downsize this home? Are we going to move to a different community? People often get so overwhelmed with how many different options they have, that they break down and do nothing.

We say to them, "Let us be your pilots. Why don't you sit comfortably in first class? We're going to take you through an exercise and ask you a lot of questions, almost like the way an architect would ask a lot of questions about a family when they are building a new house, and then out of those answers will come a subset of choices, and then you'll decide, and then we'll implement it for you."

Please share an example of how you would help somebody who had those challenges and what kind of transformational results would be able to gain for them.

David Edwards: I'm going to use our fictitious family, Frank and Joanna Miller, who are typical of our clients. They are currently 50 years old. They're 15 years to retirement. They have some money saved up, about a million so far, between their 401(k)s and their investment plans. They're living comfortably right now, but they have an expensive lifestyle. We can tell them, based on reasonable projections of investment returns and spending, that if they made no changes, they would run out of money at age 85, but we've projected them to live to be 95. So that would be a problem.

However, if you have that information 20 years in advance, you can make decisions to address that. For example, you can save more. Our financial planning platform allows us to show the effect of saving more. Or you can say, "Well, what if I work five years later?" I can click on the financial plan and show, yup, if you work five years longer, your funds will last an additional five years, to 90. Maybe that's not enough.

What if you do something like sell the vacation home and drop the vacation house expenses? Well, that extends your financial plan to age 95. That's good, but still not as comfortable as we'd like it to be. We like to go to age 100, just to be sure. Oh, but you tell us that you might inherit some money from a parent, $500,000. Well now, problem solved. You actually will have no problem lasting to 100. What if we increase annual savings anyway? Not only will you have no trouble living to 100, but you'll leave an estate of about four or five million dollars.

The most wonderful part of my job is that most people walk into our conference room at 10:30 in the morning terrified, because they don't know what's going to happen, and they're just scared to death. After we take them through this process, and show them the alternatives, and show them what they can do to make things better or worse, they walk out all smiles at 12:00. That's what our job is all about, taking fear and converting it into joy.

For those executive families who you help, please share one common, but unknown pitfall they need to be aware of, no matter what situation they find themselves in.

David Edwards: I would say one pitfall that's very common is having the wrong asset allocation. For example, some people are very leery of the stock market. They show us their 401(k) which is invested 95% in a bond fund. We would say, "No, you're not touching that money for 10 or 15 years, you can afford maximum risk in that retirement account. Let's get it to 90% equities or 100% equities or 80% equities."

Another common pitfall is having too much of their wealth in a single asset. A lot of our clients, because they're executives, have stock in the company, and they have stock options and restrictive stock. Well, that's great, but if you have, for example, 10 or $11 million in Amazon, and Amazon falls from 1400 back to 250, which we think is not unreasonable, well, you could go from $11 million in assets to $2 million in assets pretty quickly. A lot of our counseling revolves around saying to clients, "Yeah, I know you love your company. I know you hate paying capital gains tax. But let me just show you all these examples of great companies that cratered. Let's just set up a plan where we sell of 5% of the stock per quarter or per year and put the money in other securities, so if something bad does happen to your company, you still have that retirement locked in."

How many years have you been a practicing wealth advisor?

David Edwards: I started out in the early 1980s at Morgan Stanley, not in wealth management, actually in computer systems. Within a year, I was transferred to the fixed income department, mortgage-backed securities, government securities, building trading models. I did that for several years at Morgan Stanley, and then thereafter I worked as a consultant at JP

Morgan Securities and Nomura Securities building value at risk models for them. Value at risk models are very esoteric ways of measuring what can happen to a bank if markets go against them.

Eventually, I decided not to work 100 hours a week anymore, and get into a business that was a bit more family friendly. I ducked into business school for two years studying marketing operations and then started my firm within a year of graduating in 1996. When I first started the firm, I was still not a wealth manager; I was a stock picker focusing on the US midcap growth category. I focused on individual families, because without an institutional track record.

Within a few years, I found my clients asking me a lot of questions that had nothing to do with stocks and everything to do with their lifestyle. "David, what about my retirement plan? David, what about my kids' education? David, what about my divorce?" At first, I said, "Well, call your accountant, call your financial planner, call your CPA or your trust and estate attorney." But I realized that I was the guy with my hands on their money, and they wanted the answers from me.

I began to educate myself about the other aspects of wealth management. I was coming from the investment advice side. Financial planning and estate planning. Also built up a team of CFPs and CFAs, so pretty much any question a client has about their financial plan, we can answer it. On the few occasions where we feel like we don't have the best possible answer, we also bring in a network of outside advisors, perhaps life insurance salespeople, perhaps trust and estate attorneys, to make sure the client has the best possible advice at all times.

When you think back to all the clients that you've helped over the years, how does that make you feel?

David Edwards: I love my job, because if I can show somebody that everything that they would like to have their life, for their family, for their children, for their parents, for their retirement, can be delivered, and here's the plan to make it happen, is that a great job or what?

I often say, "Well, if you're a doctor, and you have to tell someone that they have cancer, that's the worst moment of their lives." Or if you're a defense attorney, and you have to tell somebody that the jury has found them guilty and they're looking at 20 years in jail. Well, that's the worst moment of their lives. I get to be with my clients at the best moments of their lives, when they retire, when they tell me about their kids' college acceptance, when we're sitting at their beach house in the Hamptons drinking margaritas, or sitting in their ski lodge in Wyoming drinking beers. Wow. What an amazing profession.

It's important for you to be able to create that transformation in your client's life then, right?

David Edwards: For sure.

What final thoughts would you like to share before we close out with our last question for today?

David Edwards: The most important thing, when you're thinking about your retirement plan, or any significant purchase in your life, is to not wait until the last minute to address it. I don't expect people to think about retirement planning in their 20s and 30s, but by the time you get to your mid-40s, early-

50s, it should be a priority. If you're not working with our firm, find another firm that is equally expert, and ask the questions, and see the results, and then make sure you follow up with the results.

If someone feels they want to know more about the glide path to retirement, what's the best way for them to connect with you?

David Edwards: They can certainly start by visiting our website, www.heron H-E-R-O-N wealth.com. We have numerous resources, videos, and guidebooks on different topics of financial planning. They can also call our 800 number, which is 800-99-H-E-R-O-N, or 800-994-3766. They can also email me directly at davidedwards@heronwealth.com

Fantastic. Let me just eliminate any doubt that anyone may have about picking up the phone and giving you a call. Briefly explain what will exactly happen when they call that number you just shared with us.

David Edwards: Sure. On the initial call, they'll speak with Anneline who's our Director of Client Experience. She will take down some basic details and set up a preliminary phone conversation. I or one of our other advisors will call back and spend half hour or 45 minutes on the phone, understanding the basics of a client's needs. If it seems like a good fit, we'll schedule them to come in for a more detailed interview in person. If they can fill out a questionnaire in advance and bring some documents, terrific. If not, we can get those later.

Eventually, we will go forward and create what we call the baseline financial plan. That's complimentary. We spend about two hours on our side pulling the basics. After that, we schedule a follow-up appointment to review the plan, the baseline plan, with both spouses. This is very important for us. Both husband and wife have to be involved in the conversation. If the prospect likes what they see, then we will ask them to review and sign our advisory agreement. The reason why we stop at that point is because this conversation is creating rights and responsibilities on both sides, and before we go further, the client needs to understand what those rights and responsibilities are.

Once we receive back the detailed advisory agreement, we go and build the detailed financial plan, followed by the detailed investment plan, followed by the onboarding process, where we bring all the assets to our custodian, Fidelity Investments in Boston. We then run the assets through our rebalancing systems, reorient the portfolio to the right asset allocation, the right mix of securities. Then we scheduled the next follow up a meeting, which is six months later, and 12 months later, and 24 months later, and as often as the client needs to speak to us.

It's not a one and done situation. It is a relationship that should last 15, 20, 25 years.

About David Edwards

David graduated from Hamilton College with a concentration in History and Mathematics and holds an MBA in General Management from Darden Graduate School of Business at the University of Virginia.

David contributed over 100 columns to TheStreet.com. He is frequently quoted in the press. David is a member of the Investment Adviser Association serving on the Legislation and Technology committees and is an advisory board member for eMoney.

Prior to founding Heron Wealth, he was associated with Morgan Stanley, JP Morgan and Nomura Securities developing investment products and quantitative trading models. David competes in sailing regattas from New England to the Caribbean and coaches a hometown team in New York Harbor.

WEBSITE

www.HeronWealth.com

EMAIL

davidedwards@heronwealth.com

LOCATION

205 East 42nd Street, 20th Floor,
New York, NY 10017

FACEBOOK

Heron Wealth

TWITTER

@HeronWealth

PHONE

(347) 580-5280

Cherie D. Morris, JD, CDC
Certified Divorce Coach

Cherie D. Morris is a Divorce Coach, Parent Coordinator, Author and Speaker who has worked for many years as a lawyer and COO of a law firm.

Cherie's experience led her to train in more holistic areas, including yoga, and to consider alternate conflict resolution as a way to avoid litigation. After her experience writing a novel, she decided, based on experience in her own life and where her skill set led her, to seek additional training to become an advocate for individuals who are either considering divorce or are anywhere in the process of divorce.

Cherie finds the ability to be a thinking partner and support to one person an amazing opportunity to help individuals make decisions in line with their best selves; a part often lost when divorce occurs. It is truly her privilege to help people make thoughtful decisions for themselves and their children in divorce.

In addition to her work with Dear Divorce Coach, Cherie is available for coaching sessions regarding divorce and other life transitions for individuals and couples too.

Conversation with Cherie D. Morris

Can you briefly describe the people you serve at Dear Divorce Coach and the kinds of situations they find themselves in when they come to you for your help?

Cherie D. Morris: Sure, at Dear Divorce Coach, we serve people who are contemplating divorce, in the midst of divorce, or who are experiencing post-divorce complications, so if divorce may either be a part of your life, is a part of your life, or there are still lingering issues from a divorce, including with children, we are here to help you, and we have lots of tools to do that.

So, keeping that in mind and obviously everything that you share with us today is not legal advice or legal assistance, can you briefly share some of the most common misconceptions surrounding communication and divorce?

Cherie D. Morris: One of the biggest misconceptions is that more communication is better than less. In fact, you really have to view your relationship with someone who was your intimate partner for perhaps a very long time, as now only a business relationship. The goal really should be to impart info in a friendly, neutral tone. Also, you should only state what you need in as few words as you can and stay on topic.

So, your goal really is to keep the communication as neutral as possible and in as few words as possible so that that person can read your letter, your email, your text if necessary, and figure out what it is you need, probably concerning your child, and act on it.

Please share an example of how you would help someone to improve their communication in divorce.

Cherie D. Morris: I think one issue I see again and again, and this can be from both men and women by the way, is a frustration with their communication because they describe to me they have told their ex again and again, their co-parent, again and again what they're doing wrong but that they are not changing. My immediate response to that is that's not likely to happen, you no longer have control over most of what they do, even with your child if you share custody of your child.

That means that it's not your job, as much as you may think you're right and frankly as right as you may be, to tell them how to do their parenting, and what that means really is the transformation has to occur not within your ex but within the person that I'm coaching.

They have to have a new mindset that they bring to discussions with their ex, so instead of framing issues as, "I will tell you what to do and what you're supposed to do," simply share information as needed and allow the parent to execute as they choose. So, really what that means in practice is deciding to communicate effectively. I help them develop a very simple three step system to do that and really bring neutrality to each of their communications with their ex, which is probably the hardest thing to do.

What are some of the communication and divorce pitfalls you'd like divorcing couples to be aware of?

Cherie D. Morris: So, I think one pitfall in particular that relates to what I just said is that you should always remember that your perspective about the issues you need to address with your ex, may not be theirs, so don't assume they view the world in the same way you do, and that if their response is not in line with your world view, that it's wrong.

So, understand your co-parent may have a very different perspective because if you can't get past that, then you may become very frustrated. Your co-parent may not be frustrated at all, and you may be spinning your wheels for a long time, needlessly wasting a lot of physical, emotional and mental energy that you'll need when moving forward with your own life. So, don't get caught. Don't get stuck by thinking that your ex needs to see the world the same way you do.

Cherie, it's a Monday morning, and your alarm goes off, you're waking up, another day ahead of you helping the people you work with, how does that feel, is it still fun for you?

Cherie D. Morris: Well, it's not only fun, but it's my joy. I feel that the work I do now is more of a mission than a career. I came to divorce coaching based on the experience of my own divorce in which (in addition to myself), had a number of good professionals such as a legal professional, a therapist, financial and even real estate people.

What I didn't have was someone to help me day by day to make the types of quick, concrete, practical decisions that come to you in divorce on a regular basis. I often describe the two year period surrounding divorce as a period of temporary insanity for most entirely rational people. It really makes sense to know you have someone walking right by your side, literally holding your hand, helping you frame those decisions and truthfully, none of the other professionals can do that.

You will pay your lawyer a very high hourly rate to do that for example, but even then, they are not necessarily well prepared to give you very practical advice in your life and certainly that's not your therapist's job either, so doing what I do brings me new challenges every single Monday, and they are ones that I really embrace.

Tell us a little bit about your background, education, and experience as it relates to effective communication in divorce.

Cherie D. Morris: My background is as you introduced me, that of a lawyer, and I think what that allows me to do is bring a real analytical framework to helping people in divorce. I have a very rational approach. I implement a lot of holistic techniques as well, but with a rational overlay. Self-care is a big part of what I do with people because until you can calm the chaos and overwhelm, you're not likely to act in a rational fashion, so I think both my lawyer background as well as my yoga teacher background come together in a manner that really serves my client well. I'm also a writer which helps me to communicate effectively with clients which in turn, helps them to communicate effectively with former spouses and co-parents too.

Also as a writer, I create articles that people can find on our website and in other outlets, that describe to people simple ways to calm the chaos, calm the overwhelm, and how they talk to children about divorce.

Almost any topic you can imagine in divorce, I try to address with my clients, so my background of the rational approach with focus upon the holistic, the self-care, the calming the chaos and overwhelm helps me, I think, to really serve my clients in a way that they need during this very difficult time.

Can you please expand on the "Three-Step System to More Effective Communication" you mentioned earlier?

Cherie D. Morris: I sure can, and although it's really simple, it's not always easy! If people listening can jot down these three steps and reflect upon them each time you need to respond to or create communication with your ex, I think it will help.

The first thing is to understand the message. What really is your co-parent asking of you? What really do you need from them? It's as simple as taking a deep breath and slowing down. If your ex is communicating forms of anger or emotional overwhelm, you don't need to respond. Keep in mind that documentation in divorce is always important, so just in case you need it sometime in the future, save it. If it doesn't need a response right away or doesn't need any response at all, put it away. That way you are not looking at it over and over again. Most importantly, take your time and take a deep breath.

Number two is to reflect upon what's happening, so before you respond you may take out their email address, and then draft the response that you want, let it be emotional, let it be cathartic, don't send, and then if you're working with me I'll ask you to send it to me and we can edit it together so that you can learn how to do that on your own, and in the meantime just wait. Then, after you've had time to reflect and edit and make it neutral, take out all that stuff that doesn't belong in the message.

Then, number three, after you've done that, remember again that you don't have to respond at all if it's just an emotional diatribe from them, if it's not and there is something to be sent, save it before sending, pause, and then send a short, neutral response.

That really will go a long way to getting the relationship you need to have with your ex. By the way, I recommend that text communication is used only in the most urgent of communications because it's simply too easy to become emotionally elevated with text messages, so unless it's a last minute logistics issue or an emergency involving your child, send an email. Give people time to reflect and don't feel that you have to respond to text messages just because they pop up on your phone.

That's a really great tip, Cherie. I too have been in several situations where I've responded to a text or WhatsApp message and totally regretted it as soon as I hit the send button.

Cherie D. Morris: Yes, we all have. It really is because of technology these days, there are so many ways to communicate and some of them, to our own detriment, as I like to tell my children too, so always think before pressing send if you can and if you can't, we all make mistakes, don't get bogged down in it but just try to remind yourself the next time to do it a little better.

Effective communication in divorce is important so you understand what your partner is saying and control your reaction to prevent more problems, right?

Cherie D. Morris: Exactly, and one of the drawbacks to that is, you can end up spending thousands of dollars in legal fees alone over a miscommunication and remember as I started with in the beginning, your ex probably doesn't share your worldview, so you can probably assume that whatever you say is not going to be seen in the generous light in which you send it. So, in knowing that, remember to back it down as much as you can to be as neutral as you can and yet have a friendly tone. Assume that they will assume the worst but really from your communication they can only get the best, and that's really the goal.

Is your role as a divorce coach to prepare people for divorce so that it goes as smoothly as possible?

Cherie D. Morris: I can do that, certainly, and in fact, one of the things that we do at Dear Divorce Coach is to help people evaluate the decision to stay in or leave their marriage. However, I can also work with them if they are already in the midst of a divorce and have found that there's a lot of chaos and overwhelm. I can help back that down and help them think about things that need to be in their agreement. I'm not giving them legal advice, but I'm certainly giving them coaching advice based on a lot of experience. Many people have complications post-divorce because they're not communicating effectively, and instead of turning to a lawyer they can simply turn to a divorce coach who can help them look at what their role in that communication may be, and how they may go back to neutral to serve themselves and their children.

The role you play can complement what a divorce lawyer does. Do the two go hand in hand in terms of preparing a couple for divorce proceedings?

Cherie D. Morris: That's a great question, and the answer is yes. In fact, I have a number of clients who work with me as they work with lawyers because the lawyer really doesn't want them to spend time with them (at their very high hourly rate), processing some of the practical issues they need to decide on. I can work with couples too if they are in a place that's very cooperative, and I also work with individuals if it's not, but my goal is always to allow them to deal with each other, especially if they have minor children because that relationship is likely one for a lifetime.

What would be your final thoughts for someone who wants to know more about effective communication during divorce?

Cherie D. Morris: Pause before hitting send. So just wait, just take a deep breath, remember that what you say to your ex matters, and how you say it matters, and that every thought you have doesn't need to be expressed, and in fact probably shouldn't be. You're allowed to have your feelings, absolutely, but it isn't necessary to communicate all of those feelings to your ex, and in fact, it won't serve your best interest or the best interest of your children to do that.

If someone wants to find out more about effective communication in divorce, how can they connect with you?

Cherie D. Morris: If people want to find out more, they're welcome to go to www.deardivorcecoach.com, or email me at cherie@deardivorcecoach.com. I also have a book available called, "Should I Stay or Should I Go?" and that's downloadable on Amazon. It has lots of good tips for you, whatever stage of divorce you're in, from contemplation to post-divorce. Feel free to take a look, and again, please reach out, we are here to help you right now.

About Cherie D. Morris

Cherie D. Morris is a Certified Divorce Coach, lawyer, yoga teacher, author and mother.

Cherie's legal training makes her approach to issues logical and reasoned. She began exploring alternative dispute resolution and mediation in order to understand how to change the nature of conflict and improve dynamics when conflict occurs, in litigation and otherwise, when a solely rational approach may not succeed. Her approach to conflict now is that rational thinking must be accompanied by the ability to empathize and compromise in order to achieve successful results.

A divorce agreement is a very important contract that requires each party to recognize, and think about, the long-term consequences of taking specific action now. She believes it is very important to understand and analyze each decision in divorce carefully, and rationally, but with a strong consideration for your best self and a relationship that may continue with a former spouse well into the future, especially when there are children involved.

Cherie had a long-term marriage, with children, which ended in divorce. This deepened her desire to explore how to make a very chaotic and stressful life transition a more organized, fair and cooperative one, when possible, in order to serve the best interests of children and adults. Cherie's training as a coach was inspired by this experience. She strongly believes, from her own and her clients' experience, that facing life transition with the support of an objective thinking partner helps clarify decisions in a supportive and accountable environment and is invaluable.

Cherie has four children of her own and is part of a blended family. She is delighted to include her partner's daughter and say they have a combined five. Life is always interesting and challenging.

WEBSITE
www.DearDivorceCoach.com

EMAIL
cherie@deardivorcecoach.com

LOCATION
3527 Winfield Ln, NW, Washington DC, 20007

FACEBOOK
Dear Divorce Coach

TWITTER
@DearDivorceTeam

PHONE
(301) 928-4695

Family Mediator and Certified Divorce Financial Analyst

Jennifer M. Segura began her college career on a path to become a psychologist. Along the way, her educational desires changed, but she still had a longing to work with families. The theory of using "peacemaking" to resolve legal issues intrigued her so much that she decided law school was the right path for me.

Throughout law school, she learned more about the mediation process and knew that was the right path which would allow her to fully embrace her passion for helping families during difficult transitions, as well as, her passion for using peacemaking in place of a destructive, cold, highly unaffordable legal process.

Jennifer obtained her law degree from Thomas Jefferson School of Law and graduated Cum Laude, trained as a family mediator and after gaining some experience mediating, opened her own firm, San Diego Family Mediation Center, in January 2009.

She has solely practiced as a family mediator since that time, and in an effort to further enhance her ability to provide her clients with the knowledge they need to stabilize their lives, she studied and became a Certified Divorce Financial Analyst™.

Conversation with Jennifer M. Segura

Can you briefly describe the kinds of people you serve and the various types of situations they find themselves in when they come to you for help?

Jennifer M. Segura: Okay. So predominantly, we are dealing with couples going through a divorce. This would be your typical married couple that would, in the past or traditionally, each go out and hire attorneys and kind of start the respective battles. So instead of ever heading out to attorneys, they start the process with us. We do offer a drop-in clinic, so they often will come to that and just kind of ask what they should do? You know, I don't even understand, what is mediation? So we give them some education on it, and it may take a couple weeks, even sometimes a couple months, and they will come back and say okay, yes, we'd like to do this. So when we are working with the divorcing couple, we are working with both partners, so they do not each take their own mediator, they each sit down with one mediator, and we do everything for them from the start through the final decree.

A small percentage of our practice is also working with premarital couples, so helping them to determine what a good prenup would be for them entering into a marriage and having the important conversations about finances that people never seem to have, as well as meeting with couples that have been married, want to stay married, but they're looking for some sort of help and assistance in keeping their marriage together that does not include counseling. So that would be some of the other little things that we do in addition to the divorce.

Keeping in mind that anything that you share with us today is not legal advice or legal assistance, briefly share one of the most common misconceptions around the topic of mediation for divorcing couples.

Jennifer M. Segura: Certainly. The top misconception that we hear is going to be that their divorce is too complex, that they couldn't possibly get through mediation because they have too much money, too many assets, too much debt, whatever the case may be. That is something that not only I think is ingrained in people but also something they hear from friends, family, maybe consulting attorneys, is that oh, no, no, your situation's far too complex. You could never do this in mediation.

What we say to them is it's absolutely not true. It has zero to do with how much money they have, how many assets they have or what the case may be. It all revolves around how much can these two work together? So, as long as these two people want to sit down, have conversations and get through these issues, and do it on their own terms rather than pursue it to a judge imposing something on them, there is nothing that can't go through mediation. We are in Del Mar, which is a very wealthy city, and all of our clients have huge net worth, and the last thing they want to do is open up that can of worms for an attorney who's going to come in and take all that money.

The only time that we possibly would say, maybe mediation's not the right place for you, is if domestic violence is involved. Now, that's not to say mediation can't work; we do have several people in town that will work with people who are high conflict, we just choose not to, but as far as the amount or value of their estate, there's nothing that we can't get through in mediation.

Please share an example of how you've helped someone who came to you with those challenges that you just described and what kind of transformational results you were able to gain for them.

Jennifer M. Segura: Sure, the baby boomers are getting to an age where we are seeing a lot more of them come into our office for divorce, and the problem often in this field is called the grey divorce. The biggest problem is that that stage in their lives, they've been married 25, 35, 40 years, they really have built their entire financial lives together, so for them to at this point in life start to divide all of this and kind of dismantle it is extremely disturbing for people in this age group.

So, what we often do is we tell them, look, we have a lot of people that will come in, and real estate is one of their biggest assets, they have several different pieces of real estate. We manage to give them the options of keeping it all together and continuing to earn money off of their estate just as they would as a married couple, but we're going to put in some safeguards, whether or not it's incorporating certain real estate or whatever the case may be for each person's needs, we tell them, we don't have to dismantle this.

Attorneys and in traditional litigation, they don't want to have any sort of connection at the end of a divorce. Whereas in mediation, if two people sitting in front of me, they're adults, they can make their own decision, and if they feel, yes, we can do this, and we can manage this in a way that both of us can survive as we had initially planned, then we're going to help them do that regardless to what mainstream litigation would say to that.

What's the most common but unknown pitfall you come across when working with divorcing couples and mediation?

Jennifer M. Segura: I would say the most common pitfall is that assuming if you walk into a litigating attorney's office, and you say, hey, I'm getting divorced, this is what I want to do, and you had approached this attorney as your attorney, to be your attorney, and they decide, oh, hey, well I could just mediate this for you. I think the biggest misconception is that a litigator who's been litigating for 20 years or whatever the case may be can litigate a case on Monday and mediate a case on Tuesday.

I just returned from an annual conference that mediators go to, it's the Academy of Professional Family Mediators, and the one thing that we are all in agreement as a profession is there is a huge difference between an attorney mediator and somebody who truly is just a mediator. The difference in that is litigators will often treat mediation as a settlement conference, and they really are not giving the clients the client determination that is so important in mediation as the whole process goes.

We want to let clients know, this is your process. We want you to determine what the outcome is. We're not here to determine what the outcome is, and we're here to support whatever outcome that is that they want, even if there may be red flags down the road, you guys still own a home jointly, that's a problem when you look through the court system. It's not a problem when you look through the mediation system., but you just have to be careful with who you choose as your mediator and just ensure that they aren't that trained as a mediator and they're not just somebody saying hey, I litigate on Monday, but tomorrow I'll be your mediator, because it's just not the same.

I just want to get a sense in your own words of your passion for what you do. It's a Monday morning, and you have a day's work ahead of you with clients who find themselves in the unfortunate position of facing a divorce. How do you feel with that kind of day ahead of you?

Jennifer M. Segura: I absolutely love meeting with clients. I guess it's one of those things that you look at people and you think, god, I'm glad that they can do that because I certainly couldn't. For example, I could look at a doctor and say I couldn't be around blood and all that kind of stuff.

I originally started my education out wanting to be a therapist, but somewhere along the line, just came into contact with mediation and the process of what it allows and kind of switched gears and went to law school, but I did go to law school with the end result being mediation, not the end result litigating and being a litigating attorney.

I absolutely have a passion for families and helping them to keep the family aspect together, even though the two people are divorcing each other, but for the children involved to maintain that family relationship and to maintain a friendship and a co-parenting relationship. There's nothing more satisfying than starting with a couple who are really not getting along to the end of the process where they're friends again, and we've helped to take them on a journey to remember what it was about each other that they fell in love with in the first place to at least get them back to a common ground and respect for each other.

My clients call me years later to come back if they ever have any parenting arrangements they want to change or any issues that pop up, they're calling me six, seven, eight years later, which helps me to realize I really am making a difference in their life. They're not heading to court; they're coming back to me. It's a great feeling, and I love what I do, and I love being with my clients and helping them create healthy, ongoing relationships.

Please share a little bit more about your background, your education, and the experience you have with divorce mediation.

Jennifer M. Segura: I did go to law school. I came to San Diego for my undergrad, went to SDFU, I was an English major and went to law school here in San Diego as well. About halfway through, did some mediation training, realized I really enjoyed it. I did work in some law firms through law school, but by the end, realized I definitely enjoyed the mediation aspect and the process. So became officially trained in mediation.

Shortly after law school in January of 2008, I opened up this practice. A couple years after that, I also became trained as a certified divorce financial analyst because it became very evident that the two main things in a divorce, it's going to be your finances and your children, and there's really nothing else there, those are the two things that we're working with.

So, I've made it a point to keep myself very relevant with any kind of changes in the finances and different ways that we can create support and assets and distributions to help the family, not only the day they walk out of my office, but five years, 10 years, 15 years down the road trying to set them up for success at the end of this and not for struggling and having to come back in and having to go to court to change things.

Two years ago, I took on a partner, her name is Amanda Singer, and she also has a law background and also a Masters of Dispute Resolution from Pepperdine here in California, and both of us just share the same passion of wanting to change the way that divorce is handled, at least here in California.

Hopefully people will start to model what we can show them and that the success rate in couples following the agreements that are made is so much higher when they are part of putting the agreement together, and the agreement is what they want and what's best for their family instead of being pushed through this cookie-cutter system of civil court, which is never meant to deal with families. So, it's something that we both hope to change as the years go by.

Divorce rates are unfortunately on the increase. Is divorce mediation a trend?

Jennifer M. Segura: I really think it is. Again, as I said, we just came back from a conference when we spend time with the actual founding people in mediation, which happened about 35, 40 years ago, which is amazing to think, because it's really taken this long for it to become more mainstream.

But nowadays, we have people sit down in our office, and the first thing out of their mouth is, we do not want attorneys involved. They do not want them involved, because they know that it's a corrupt system that is geared to take their money and the more controversy and the more that the pot can be stirred, the more money that the professionals involved are going to make.

We work in a much more collaborative effort and what we do is when we do have couples come in, if there are any issues or if either party is very concerned about the legalities or anything else, we encourage them to get a consulting attorney, but to work with them just as a consulting attorney, not as their representing attorney. We often will hook them together with CPA's or CFP's or other people that may be needed in order to educate them or for them to gain a better understanding of what the finances have been throughout the marriage and what that means for them going forward.

For either partner who has been home and not out in the workforce, trying to help them get reestablished, and what is that going to take, and helping them to figure out what do they want to do and getting both parties on board with whatever that journey is. Because at the end of that journey now that person's going to be self-supporting.

So, let's support them to get there so that you're not supporting them for the rest of your life. We really take a holistic approach with our clients and try to help them in every aspect of their life and not just this one little part, but we try to help them overall for a new fresh start.

Any final thoughts?

Jennifer M. Segura: Just to keep in mind that always start with mediation. That if there is some reason that it won't work that litigation is always there. It's always there, but you should always think of litigation as a last resort, instead of the first call you make. The way that the divorce starts, the tone that it starts in is typically going to be the tone that is carried out throughout the process. So, if one of you head off and hire an attorney and serve the other party and start off in a very contentious way, the chances are that's what your process is going to look like for the duration of the divorce.

That's not healthy, it's not healthy for either party, it's not healthy for the children, and it's something that takes years to get through. With mediation, we can get people through it quick, efficient, in a friendly way, in a positive way, so just keep in mind to start with mediation. If it doesn't work, there's always the opportunity to go the other direction. But this is something that I think can work with anybody that's looking to do mediation. I think absolutely; you can do it if you want to do it.

If somebody finds themselves in that unfortunate position of being divorced, what's the best way to find you?

Jennifer M. Segura: You can find us on the web at www.sandiegofamilymediation.com. Also, you can email me at jen@sandiegofamilymediation.com. Or our telephone number is 858-736-2411. We do also have a fantastic blog on our website, so if you are just looking for information, definitely check out our blog. We do update it weekly. So, we always are putting out as much information as we can to help educate the public.

About Jennifer M. Segura

Jennifer is the founder and principal mediator of the San Diego Family Mediation Center, located in Del Mar, California.

Her primary goal is to educate people about the benefits of mediation, not only in family law matters but in all matters. She has been mediating divorces for over 9 years and absolutely loves her job.

Specialties: Family mediation, including pre-marital contracts, post-marital contracts, dissolution of both marital and non-marital relationships, parenting coordination, and probate matters. Mediations are generally completed using only one mediator. However, team mediation will be provided upon request.

WEBSITE
www.SanDiegoFamilyMediation.com

EMAIL
Jen@SanDiegoFamilyMediation.com

LOCATION
2002 Jimmy Durante Blvd. Suite 122,
Del Mar, CA 92014

FACEBOOK
San Diego Family Mediation Center

TWITTER
@SDFMC

PHONE
(619) 840-5992

San Diego Family Mediation Center

Amanda D. Singer, Esq, MDR, CDFA is a proud co-owner and family mediator of San Diego Family Mediation Center. Amanda is dedicated to helping families deal with conflict constructively, finding ways to improve communication, solve problems, and reach agreements on legal and non-legal issues. She has seen litigation destroy relationships and is passionate about the mediation process, which helps her clients maintain a relationship and get to the heart of the issues that are causing conflict.

Amanda helps families through all stages of life including pre-marital mediation, marital mediation, divorce mediation, parenting plans, blended family mediation, and estate planning distribution. Her goal is to help educate people on the benefits of mediation and to see how she can help.

Amanda has a JD from Chapman University School of Law as well as a Masters in Dispute Resolution from The Straus Institute of Dispute Resolution at Pepperdine University School of Law, and has completed extensive mediation training, including certification as a Certified Divorce Financial Analyst (CDFA™) and is thrilled to continue serving the great community of San Diego!

Conversation with Amanda D. Singer

Can you describe the people you serve and the situations they find themselves in when they come to you for help?

Amanda D. Singer: Certainly. I work with couples who are going through family conflicts, especially divorce and they want to stay out of court, and usually they want to work together using a neutral third party such as myself as a mediator.

We find that they're usually at the beginning steps in a divorce process. Most of the time they are not quite sure how they're going to handle the whole divorce process and have yet to hire attorney's and are looking for an alternative situation because they know that they don't want to fight things out in court and spend all the money that comes along with hiring an attorney, but they're not always sure what the other options are.

They usually want to keep their cost down because going through a divorce can be an expensive process for anyone, such as figuring out how they're going to live in two separate households. They want to know up front what it's going to cost and they also know that they don't want to hate each other at the end of the process.

So, we find that some of the couples that come to us, they might agree on somethings, but quite often, I get people who don't agree on anything except for the fact that they know they want to come in for mediation. So, they may be still fighting and may argue in my office, but they know it's a better route.

They often have various issues, such as putting together a parenting plan, coming up with support issues, and dividing the property that they own together and figuring out how they're going to move forward, get everything done on the legal side as well as emotionally work out their issues with their spouse.

Please share a common misconception you come across while helping your clients on a day to day basis.

Amanda D. Singer: I think a common misconception that I see, especially as it relates to maintaining a positive co-parenting relationship, is that even though you're no longer married to your spouse, it doesn't mean that you have to hate each other and in fact when there are kids involved you can still maintain a positive co-parenting relationship for your kids and do what's going to be best for them in the situation. So I think that people sometimes think just because we're not married that we don't know how we can do this and still remembering that you're a family and you have kids together and you need to maintain some kind of relationship for them.

Can you share an example of how you've helped someone who came to you with those challenges that you just described and what kind of transformational results you were able to gain for them?

Amanda D. Singer: Yeah, certainly. So, I think that one of the situations that come to mind is of a couple I worked with in mediation. That one spouse had an affair in this situation, and so the trust was lost between the two of them.

That can a lot of times cause issues moving forward from learning to co-parent together and really trusting that person again, but realizing for the kids; they have to do that. So I think what we did in mediation is to be able to have an open conversation that has nothing to do with who's at fault and what happened in the divorce and focusing solely on the kids as the main focus and being able to work out a schedule.

In this situation, they really wanted mom to stay in the house with the kids. So being able to work out a situation where mom could be in the house with the kids, but both parents would still be involved.

And being able to both see the kids, especially these days, we find that kids are involved in so many different activities that in this situation we were able to make sure that both mom and dad were going to attend baseball and soccer games and gymnastics practice, and be there for the kids and that it didn't matter whose day it was.

It didn't matter if it was moms weekend, dad was still able to work together and be there for the kids, knowing that the kids always come first and additionally understanding that there may be new partners, and even in this situation the one that had been involved in the affair had that person in their life still, but understanding that the kids come first, and it doesn't matter how you might feel about the other parent, but they still have to put their children first.

What is the most common but unknown pitfall that you'd like to bring to their attention today?

Amanda D. Singer: So, I think one of the common pitfalls is not having a strong foundation to build and maintain a positive co-parenting relationship that really goes to the heart of why we do mediation, and why mediation is going to be a better option for people to avoid this pitfall. Litigating pits each party against each other. It doesn't allow you to want to work with your spouse when the process is over because you may be in the court process for years and the things are brought up in court really only turns you against the other spouse, and it is just acrimonious in its nature.

Mediation, on the other hand, brings the two co-parents together to establish a healthy parenting plan for both the parents and the children, and it really allows them to start off from the point of resolving their conflicts amicably and having that foundation such that if the children are four and six now, as they get older we've already started with a solid beginning, and we know that form there the parents are going to be able to work together throughout their children's lives and not just until they turn 18, but beyond that as well.

Can you tell us about your education, background, and how it all relates to the topic of family law?

Amanda D. Singer: I am, as you said at the beginning, a professional family mediator, but I am also a licensed attorney and a Certified Divorce Financial Analyst. I have both my law degree as well as, a master's in dispute resolution and pretty extensive mediation training.

I've been working as a family mediator for over five years, and I've my own practice along with my partner, Jennifer for over two years now. Because of my education and experience in conflict resolution, the law, and finances, it really allows me to work with couples through all aspects of divorce and really understand what they need assistance with and most importantly the extensive understanding of conflict and dispute resolution because I'm really able to understand the conflicts that brought them to my office, but also want to work with them to move past that and help them learn how to resolve their future conflicts amicably and maintain that co-parenting relationship.

I think that a lot of times when you're working with an attorney, or when you're working with a mediator, or financial professional, they're not really thinking about what comes next. I grew up with my mom who was a therapist, and saw that there's the emotional side of relationships and going through a divorce, but also the practical problem solving of how do you move forward and how do you get from where you are now to a spot where you feel comfortable with your co-parent, and you're able to work together.

If someone wants to know more about maintaining a positive co-parenting relationship and how to resolve future conflicts amicably with their ex-spouse, how would they be able to connect with you?

Amanda D. Singer: We always offer a free consultation where I am always happy to talk with them. Just call I can (858) 736-2411. I can also be easily found online at www.sandiegofamilymediation.com or via under my name Amanda Singer on LinkedIn.

About Amanda D. Singer

Growing up, Amanda's mom was a therapist, and she learned early on how important feelings can be to relationships and that people need to tell other people how they feel, or they won't know what needs to be changed. Amanda had originally thought about following her mom's footsteps and becoming a therapist but was also interested in law and problem-solving

During her senior year in college at Brandies University, Amanda took one of her last classes for her legal studies minor on mediation, negotiation and conflict resolution. This class is what really turned her on to mediation and made her realize that there was a career option that would allow her to blend the emotional side of conflict with pragmatic problem-solving.

She only applied to schools that had dispute resolution programs so that she could not only get her law degree but also take classes in mediation and conflict resolution. Determined not to be in graduate school for longer than three years, she worked on completing her JD at Chapman University School of Law while earning her Masters in Dispute Resolution (MDR) from The Straus Institute of Dispute Resolution and Pepperdine University School of Law. While completing both degrees, Amanda was able to learn more about the law, how people deal with conflict and ways to resolve it.

WEBSITE
sdfmc.com

EMAIL
amanda@sandiegofamilymediation.com

LOCATION
2002 Jimmy Durante Blvd. Suite 122
Del Mar, CA 92014

FACEBOOK
San Diego Family Mediation Center

TWITTER
@SDFMC

LINKEDIN
San Diego Family Mediation Center

CFP, CDFA™ Transitions Planner

Adrienne Rothstein Grace has a wealth of experience in the area of financial divorce and brings 30 years of financial advisory experience to clients in transition. Whether that transition is in marital status, household partners, job change or elder year planning, Adrienne's holistic approach to financial transition planning guides clients through prudent preparation as well as rebuilding.

With a measured approach to growth and preservation of assets, Adrienne works closely with her clients to develop a sound, comprehensive plan, created for each individual in transition. Adrienne's focus is to help clients navigate their transition eliminating financial pitfalls.

Besides being emotionally draining, divorce is financially unsettling as well. Dividing income and assets into two households can be a challenging process. Financial Planners have traditionally worked with individuals after divorce, helping them build new lives and plan for their future. By being uniquely qualified to make long-term financial projections, Divorce Financial Planners integrate the methodology of financial planning directly into the divorce process.

Adrienne explains her client's options, help them to set priorities, leads them through the hard choices ahead. She examines and analyzes the financial issues of their divorce, and provides individuals (and their attorneys) with data to help them make informed decisions while trying to bring peace of mind to a difficult and emotional process.

Conversation with Adrienne Rothstein Grace

Can you just briefly describe the people who you serve and the kind of situations they find themselves in when they come to you for help?

Adrienne Rothstein Grace: Well, the people that I work with are either contemplating divorce, or they're faced with that decision in front of them. They are usually the spouse who did not manage the finances of the marriage, and they have very high anxiety about their financial security during and after the divorce. I help them understand their financial situation and negotiate better settlements that they can live with now and later. Because, as we unfortunately know, marriage is about love and divorce is about money.

Keeping that in mind that anything you share with us today is not legal advice or legal assistance, can you share some of the most common misconceptions surrounding the financial ramifications of divorce?

Adrienne Rothstein Grace: Well, often there are several issues among the most common misconceptions or mistakes that are made, one of the is not considering the long-term effect of a negotiated settlement.

When our lawyers do a great job in helping our clients to negotiate and come down to the bottom line, they will often stop at that point. When the documents are signed, the lawyer's job is done. Often, unfortunately, we find that while the settlement may be good for now, it may not work down the road.

There may be other financial situations that should've been taken into consideration and may have been missed. One of the most frequent issues that I see is often the spouse who is responsible for the children; often the wife will keep the house in exchange for the retirement plan.

She'll often say, "Well I promised him that he could have his retirement plan. After all, he may have worked for that while I was home with the kids. I'll just keep the house." That is not always a good situation, and can, unfortunately, come back to be something that she may regret.

Share an example of how you've helped someone who came to you with those challenges and what kind of results you were able to achieve for them.

Adrienne Rothstein Grace: I did have a client who came in and said exactly that. "I've been home with the kids. He's been out working and earning the retirement plan, and I promised him that he could have it." What I suggested to her was that perhaps that might be what came out in the end, but wouldn't it be a lot better to understand what his pension or retirement plan was actually worth? That way, we would be able to make a more informed decision. We did the research, looked into it, and determined that the value of the plan was about three times as much as the value of the house.

We were able to use that information and negotiate a much better, I'd call it a deal, but a much better value for her, where they split the equity in the house, and they split the value of the pension. That was enough for her to buy a right-sized house for herself and the children, and give her a fresh start with some extra cash. Some retirement funds for her, for the future.

It's so easy to forget that the decisions that are made now are irrevocable in most cases. You don't get a do-over. Whatever you decide right now is what it's going to be. I want to make sure that I can help my clients have as much information to make that right decision. To make that informed decision with confidence, that it'll work for them now and later on too.

That client that you just mentioned sounded almost as if she was passive, saying, "Hey, it's okay. He can have it." Is that something you come across on a regular basis?

Adrienne Rothstein Grace: I come across this all the time. The negotiation in a divorce is really a reflection of what the relationship may have been between husband and wife during the marriage.

Often, even now, there's still a division of labor in the household, especially when you have young kids, and where the choice has lovingly been made for the wife to stay home with the children. I see that so often with highly compensated professional men, who make a lot of money.

After all, in our hearts as women, it may be our dream to stay home and be Mom. In doing that, they often give up knowledge of the finances of the household and come into a pattern, again particularly with highly compensated professional men who are used to making decisions. So there comes to be a dynamic where what he says goes.

If he's the one who's controlling the checkbook or controlling the flow of money, the intimidation factor can be there, either overtly or covertly. We often would prefer just not to have that high level of conflict. Just say, "Well, whatever you want. I need to be out of this. I don't want to subject the children to that kind of conflict, or myself."

One of the main things that I suggest to my clients, and it's my absolute best piece of advice, is to form a team. Going through a divorce is such a major life event, you don't need to do it alone. My ideal component of a team is, you need an attorney to provide the legal information. In a litigated case, you may either go through an attorney where both parties hire attorneys and go to court, or you may choose a mediator that can help you come to an agreement out of court.

There's also a third choice, and that's called Collaborative Law. In Collaborative Law, all the professionals have been trained to help people come to agreement out of court. It's a much more respectful procedure. It's generally less expensive and really helps to keep the conflict level down, so that people can come to agreement rather than having to fight over everything.

Whichever way you choose, everyone should have a lawyer for legal advice. Perhaps they may use a mediator to help them come to an agreement. I really, really urgently suggest to my clients that they see a therapist or a counselor, just for advice perhaps during this time period.

Divorce is emotional. Having a therapist or a mental health counselor can help people get over some of those emotional issues that can stall negotiations, and can really raise the level of conflict beyond what it needs to be.

What are some of the most common mistakes people make when it comes to the financial ramifications of divorce?

Adrienne Rothstein Grace: Most people don't consider that whenever we find ourselves in tax time, and we're approaching the deadline for filing income taxes, Uncle Sam is always going to be hidden participant in their divorce settlements.

Alimony is taxable to the recipient, and it's a tax deduction to the person who's paying it. That's a benefit to the payer, but many people who are going to be receiving alimony forget to calculate the tax bill, to get to what the net cash is really going to be.

In addition, when people talk about taking pro-investment accounts and then liquidating them to provide more money to buy another house, or just pay regular expenses, when there are profits in those accounts, selling them generates a tax bill on the profits, as well as other tax issues which can arise from joint tax returns. That is a very major issue. That's why I play that role often in divorce negotiations and helping people realize and plan for what the tax implications may be.

Could you tell us a little bit about your background, your education, and the experience you have as it relates to the topic of divorce.

Adrienne Rothstein Grace: I've done a lot in financial services. Actually, I think I've done everything over a long career. I've been a banker, I've been a teller, I've been a trust officer. I've been an investment professional and a financial planner, and my background is in teaching adults.

Around 2010, I had three women in a row come into my wealth management practice. Each of them had a funky issue about the finances of their divorce that had not been handled properly. Now, I'm both divorced and widowed, and so I'm familiar with the process. Of course, I was the financial person, so that was not the major issue in my divorce.

When I was talking to them, I realized what a huge area of anxiety this is. How little people often know about how money really works, and how much you need support during that divorce process. It's now my joy and my privilege to help people make sense out of the finances of their divorce, support them as they go through the process, and then help them rebuild after.

Is your work something that you really enjoy? When you wake up every day, is it still something that you really look forward to?

Adrienne Rothstein Grace: I love this work, I really do. I'm so thrilled that, as an entrepreneur, I realize that I get to choose what area I work in, and this is my choice. When I initially see a client, they are often weepy and small and disempowered. They're at the low point of their lives. It's part of the joy of what I do, to help them come through that. To gain information, to gain knowledge, to gain confidence. To rebuild themselves into either who they used to be, or who they'd rather be, and really see that transformation. That's what runs me.

What would you like to share with someone that is preparing for the financial ramifications of divorce?

Adrienne Rothstein Grace: You don't have to do this alone. Experts are out there; professionals are out there to help you through the process. Take advantage of them. As I said before, form that team. A lawyer, a therapist, a financial advisor, particularly a certified divorce financial analyst at this particular time. They can help you get through this process with confidence, and with the knowledge that you're doing the very best that you can for yourself and your children.

We've spoken about the misconceptions, some of the pitfalls. You have shared some great information about mistakes and your background. I understand that you recently launched a book. Are some of the topics that we've spoken about today covered in the book?

Adrienne Rothstein Grace: Absolutely. The book is called, "Going from We to Me: A Financial Guide to Divorce."

In the book, I touch on all the topics that we've talked about today, and lots more. Although names and circumstances have been altered, I use vignettes, little stories about my clients, to illustrate each of the issues that come up in the course of a divorce. I think it's very readable, my friends and clients have told me that it is. It's my pleasure to have it up available on Amazon.com, for anyone who would wish to purchase it.

If somebody out there who wants to know more about how to prepare for the financial ramifications of divorce, how would they be able to connect with you?

Adrienne Rothstein Grace: Okay. Well, my email is adrienne@adriennegrace.com. I have a website, which is www.transitioningfinances.com. If anyone would like to call me for further information, they're certainly welcome to do so. My number is (716) 817-6425.

About Adrienne Rothstein Grace

Through her 30 years of experience, Adrienne Rothstein Grace had developed a focused specialty of guiding clients through the many financial hurdles they face when in transition. That transition can be the result of a myriad of life changes from divorce or death of a loved one, to disability.

Her background in every area of financial services, coupled with extensive training and multiple professional licenses and designations, allows her to assist people to understand their financial position, organize their assets and liabilities, make better financial decisions during their time of transition, and advise on investment and management of assets to rebuild their financial lives.

When the legal work is accomplished, Adrienne's skills help the client move on.

WEBSITE
http://transitioningfinances.com

EMAIL
adrienne@adriennegrace.com

FAX
716-313-1754

LOCATION
1404 Sweet Home Rd #9
Buffalo, NY 14228

You Don't Have to Just Get By

*How to Change Your Mindset About Financial
Success and Design the Life That You Want*

Are you working full time, but still struggling with your finances? When you look at your bank account at the end of the month, do you find yourself wondering where all your money went? Do you often have the feeling that your money is just vaporizing? Is your spending out of control, but you don't know how to bring it under control? Are your debt levels high? If you answered yes to one or all of these questions, you're probably one of the millions of people who are tired of living paycheck to paycheck but just can't figure out how to get out of that cycle.

Even if you can't identify with any of the questions above, you might still find yourself struggling to reach your financial goals. You may not be drowning in debt, but no matter how much pinching and saving you do, you find that you still can't get ahead financially and achieve the big goals that you've set for yourself.

Regardless of what group you find yourself in and regardless of how your financial goals may vary, adjusting your mindset and shifting your worldview are the first steps towards making money and saving money. Get ready to enter a world where you can change your life by implementing strategies that will help you accumulate assets and build passive income. With the assistance of a seasoned wealth management coach, you can gain the skills and knowledge to build multiple streams of income. You can learn how to recognize and take advantage of opportunities that will allow you to decouple yourself from a paycheck and start creating income from other sources.

If you want to start accumulating assets, investing, and growing your cash flow so you don't have to depend on your job as your only source of income, take a few moments and discover how building multiple streams of income can help provide you the life that you want.

Conversation with Ty Robinson

What is your company's name?

Ty Robinson: It's Promethean Education LLC.

How long have you been in business?

Ty Robinson: A little over a year and a half now. I've been doing wealth strategy work for years but decided to become official because we were building a lot of products and services.

Can you share about wealth strategy and what you do?

Ty Robinson: Wealth strategy is a little different than a financial adviser. Financial advisers are licensed, and they recommend assets. They'll say, "Oh, you should go buy stock XYZ" or "Put your money here." You give them your money and they just kind of put it in whatever they want, whatever they think is best for you. Wealth strategy involves a bit more education. It's about teaching people how to manage their own finances because no one cares more about your money than you. No one's ever going to care more about your money than you. That's just a fact.

In 30 years, as we've seen from the past financial crisis, a lot of times when you want to retire, and you've given your money to the financial industry, it's not there when you need it. Some people want a little more control over their money. They're more like do-it-yourself type of people and wealth strategy gives them the knowledge and the tools to go out and pick their own assets, manage their own money instead of giving it away, and they know how to do that in the optimal way. For example, anyone can go buy stocks or index funds nowadays, but there are optimal strategies for actually buying things of that nature. That's what wealth strategy encompasses.

How can people stop living paycheck to paycheck without getting a second job?

Ty Robinson: It's about building a base of assets. That's what rich people do. The average multi-millionaire has several different streams of income, whereas the average middle-class person has just one, which is their job. If you're middle class and have one stream of income, you're very susceptible to economic and financial shocks. If your company downsizes or if the economy goes into recession, then your income is automatically placed at risk. But if you have several streams of income, you can have some of those streams go away and still have much less risk. You're still making money.

Those income streams could be rental property. It could be dividend stocks. It could be peer to peer investments. There are all kinds of different things that are available and a lot of those are passive. They are streams that will create income without you really working. Rental property is one good example of a passive income asset. If you buy a rental property and hand it off to a manager, they will manage the property for you, and you just get the checks deposited into your bank account. Eventually those passive streams of income can replace your paycheck. A lot of people retire under their passive income. So, the goal of having several streams of income is to decouple yourself from the necessity of your paycheck, and there are a lot of strategic ways you can go about doing that.

What are the advantages of working with you to achieve passive income streams?

Ty Robinson: Well, many people ask, "How do I have money to invest in a passive income stream?" So, I start off from a very basic level - a cause. I find that a lot of people, as I mentioned earlier, don't really know where all their money is going. They think they do because when you talk to the average person, they're like, "Oh yeah, I know what I'm spending my money on right now," or "I know how much I have going into savings every month." But most of the time what I see is that people don't actually know with a high level of accuracy where their money is going. They sort of have a leaky ship. No matter how much they try to invest, the ship is leaking from the bottom and it's very hard to get ahead that way.

So, we would start by finding the money. And a lot of people, once they start doing automatic spending tracking and getting a handle on the basics of their finances, they're able to find a lot of extra income that they didn't know they had and that can be applied towards building your asset base. That's where we start most of the time.

What do you feel are the biggest myths out there that you've heard when it comes to getting out of debt and earning additional income? Can you speak to some of those myths?

Ty Robinson: Everyone's situation is a little different. Everyone's strategy is a little different. But one myth is that you should invest in your 401(k) for the long-term. Everyone is taught this by the financial industry because the financial industry has a clear benefit to teaching this. They say, "Oh, you can work at your job for 30 years, save money in your 401(k), and then you'll have enough to retire." But only one in three Americans is able to retire on what they've saved in their 401(k). Even if you are able to retire, there are so many fees that you pay over the course of those 30 years that you end up losing tons of money in those fees. At the end of 30 years, if you don't have enough for retirement, the financial industry already made their money off of you and they don't really care. They don't have skin in the game. They're not taking any risks. So, that's one myth.

Another myth is the myth of autopilot where you can rely on the financial industry and trust that everything is going to be fine. But the truth is that for a lot of people, especially for baby boomers who are retiring or trying to retire, they're going to have a hard time. The autopilot myth is made up of this mentality that we can just hand our money over to someone else and it would magically be fine, but for most of human history that hasn't been the case. I mean, you really have to be on top of your own nest egg.

What are some misconceptions around how to make money passively that you've heard?

Ty Robinson: There is a lot of generalization out there. One, for example, is that if you go and buy some rental property, you can make passive income and replace your paycheck. But as there is with any investment strategy, there are a lot of nuances to buying rental property. As with buying a stock for example, it's wise to be sure that you're buying it at the best time. You have to be sure that it's a good company and you can't determine that from something you heard on the news or from somebody that says XYZ is a good company.

There are a lot of people investing just because of what their friends are doing or because of things that they've heard or because of something they've read, but they don't really know much about it. They're allocating capital - their hard-earned money - into these assets and they don't really know what they're doing. That misconception is the misconception of, "Oh, I've seen other people have success doing this, so I'll do it and get the same results." We've seen that recently with Bitcoin.

Good advice. What are some of the most common fears you've seen people have about talking to someone like yourself about their finances?

Ty Robinson: Fear is one of the most powerful drivers in the human psyche and it can be a strong motivator for someone to do the wrong thing. In fact, it can be a strong barrier to doing anything. So, a lot of people have, of course, the fear of loss. They're worried about losing all their money. There's the fear of not knowing enough and having a lack of financial education; so, they'll say, "Well, I don't know anything about it. I'm not going to do anything. I'm not going to put any money in. A lot of financial management and wealth building is about pushing through these fear barriers, especially those common ones - the fear of loss and the fear of not understanding what you're doing. Both of those things have mitigators that we teach. For example, there are ways to limit your losses. There are ways to quickly learn what you need to know in order to invest safely.

It starts with a good educational foundation, so they understand how it works and then it's really about taking action in baby steps. Once you get your feet wet, so to speak, it's much easier to swim, instead of just jumping in the pool. Taking action is a really powerful way to eliminate fear but you just want to do it in a safe controlled environment - an environment, in fact, that they control because they're controlling their own money, they're making the decisions, but they're doing it with a coach. So, it's much safer.

What other perceived obstacles do you see that might be preventing people from seeking the help of a wealth management coach?

Ty Robinson: There are those who think that they're not making enough money because a lot of financial advisers will only work with people who have a certain amount of assets. This is because most advisers get paid on commissions. There's also the issue of trust which is a big one. Business, as they say, moves at the speed of trust. So, it's important that you trust whoever you're working with, especially when they're teaching you about financial things. If you think about it, with financial advisers, you're actually giving a stranger your money. With a coach, however, you always have control of your own money. You're not giving it to anyone else.

With regard to the perceived obstacle that they don't make enough money, is there a minimum amount that someone has to make to work with you or do they need to have a minimum amount of investments?

Ty Robinson: There's no minimum because it's all based on foundational education. We see people all the time who are living paycheck to paycheck. They have almost nothing with which to invest but after going through the program, they find a lot more money that they didn't know they had and are able to turn their entire financial picture around. There is the first tier we offer, that's a great place to start for people in that category.

Then, for the coaching tier, we kind of like to see people have a free cash flow of at least around $500 to $1,000 a month. Free cash flow being how much you actually have available to put into the bank after you've paid your rent, your food and all your bills. A lot of people get there by starting with the foundational part and getting their spending under control. Once they do that, they can jump to the higher tier and start doing much bigger things.

Can you speak briefly to common mistakes you see people living paycheck to paycheck make?

Ty Robinson: A lot of people don't set financial goals and if they do have such goals, they're not sure why they have them. So, they end up not completing anything. I see that a lot because you need a strong WHY to pull you to reach your financial goals. For example, if you have a big goal such as wanting to buy a house, you can't have a willy-nilly reason for doing it. Otherwise, you're not going to go through the difficulty, the ups and downs, and the sacrifice it takes to buy a house. A lot of my clients want to own their house free and clear in a short amount of time and that takes a lot of discipline.

On the flip side, another mistake is feeling like you can't achieve any financial success and so they don't even bother, and that's where a lot of the out of control spending comes from. They think: I'll never be able to buy a house so I'm going to go buy a brand-new car.

Can you share a success story of how you have helped someone who thought your services couldn't help them?

Ty Robinson: Yes. I had a client who technically was not living completely paycheck to paycheck, but he had a lot of credit card debt. He was kind of underwater with his credit card debt and couldn't see any way out of it. We put him in our foundational program here at Promethean and got his credit card debt paid off really quick. We changed his whole mindset about money. His previous mindset about money had him falling into a large amount of debt. As his debt increased, his net income decreased. So, even though he didn't start out living paycheck to paycheck, he was on that road. The credit card debt just kept building like a snowball. We showed him that by accumulating assets, those assets, and the cash flow that comes with them, instead could accumulate like a snowball. It really opened his eyes to what was possible, and he went from that really tough situation to buying his first property and then paying off that property in five years by using the foundational skills that he learned. He then acquired a second property and now is on to his third property.

What inspired you to help people eliminate bad debt and invest in passive income opportunities or provide opportunities for passive income investments?

Ty Robinson: Helping people to succeed financially is a high for me, especially when I can get them to change their mindset. It's fun and exciting to see people acquire assets and see their passive income grow, but the most fun is seeing them go from where they are today to where they want to be. Watching the person change is a lot of fun. It's not so much of the wallet change or the bank account change, it's seeing them become a better person - the person who they wanted to become, who they needed to become in order to achieve their goals. That's the fun part for me.

Can you share a lesson you learned early on that still impacts you and how you do business today?

Ty Robinson: I think early on I focused a lot on systems. I thought that the core problem was that people didn't know how to do things. I had the idea that if you just teach them the math and the nuts and bolts of how to do something, they're just going to do it and they're going to be fine. That thinking turned out to be completely false. I learned that 90% is the mindset of people and I learned that the hard way. I was trying to help people with the nuts and bolts and it just wasn't working. They couldn't get why they were doing it.

Their motivation was extremely low. I was like, "Why aren't you motivated to make money? Doesn't everyone want to make money?" But, shockingly, if you don't have the right mindset, you really don't want to make money. You don't want to achieve success. That's a crazy thing to say, but that's what I learned. One of the most impactful things that I learned about helping people was to start with the paradigm.

What's the most important question people should ask themselves to get off the hamster wheel and stop living paycheck to paycheck?

Ty Robinson: The root question is not an easy question to answer and it's not an easy question to be introspective about. But the question is this: Can you step back from your day to day and really dig deep inside and examine if the beliefs that you have about the world, the beliefs that you have about money, are helping you get towards your goals or are they getting in the way?

One way to think about it is to pick someone who is successful that you admire. How would they look at it? How would they look at this particular view of money or view of success? Is it helping or is it hurting? If you find beliefs that are helping you, hold on tight to those. But if you find one that's not helping you, you have to work towards getting rid of it and replacing it with one that will.

How can someone determine if they need a wealth management coach or professional?

Ty Robinson: If you're struggling with your finances, then you need a wealth management coach. If you're not reaching your financial goals fast enough, then you could use a wealth management coach.

What closing thought would you like to leave someone with who is tired of getting by?

Ty Robinson: You don't have to just get by. The tools and the knowledge are out there to design the life that you want. Everyone can. So why not you? Why not now?

How can someone find out more about you and your wealth management strategy?

Ty Robinson: They can find me online at tyrobinson.com.

About Ty Robinson

Ty Robinson is an Investor, Advisor, Wealth Strategist and Entrepreneur. He is a production consultant in the Virtual and Augmented Reality industries. As a Wealth Strategist, he helps employees and freelancers implement strategies to increase monthly passive income, rapidly pay off debt, and align their finances with their lifestyle and most important goals. Ty has also authored several eBooks including *Crypto Profits*, an introduction to the cryptocurrency revolution.

Ty has been investing for 20 years with a focus on real estate holds and flips, P2P investments and cryptocurrency.

Previously, Ty worked in the video game and animation industries, working on games such as *Dance Dance Revolution*, *TMNT* and *Star Wars Star Fighter* as well as animated TV commercials for Bell South and Motif Wines. Ty has also produced two animated films, "Haloa" and "Maisa", which have screened in film festivals around the world.

After going out on his own, he started a software company specializing in software engineering for the video game industry, primarily serving the Asia market. Some of the company's key clients were Sanrio, Outblaze and MXR Corp. Ty has also owned an animation company which worked on films and commercials as well as two series pilot episodes.

Ty attended the Academy of Art University and majored in 3D Animation. He received his MBA from the University of Liverpool.

WEBSITE

www.liquidfw.com (B2B)

www.liquidfw.com/p/liquidstrategy (B2C)

FACEBOOK

www.facebook.com/tykeirobinson

TWITTER

www.twitter.com/iamtyrobinson

LINKEDIN

www.linkedin.com/in/robinsonty